INNOVATIONS IN PRODUCT TRAINING

INNOVATIONS IN PRODUCT TRAINING

Strategies for Success

Debra J. Smith

iUniverse, Inc.
New York   Bloomington

Innovations in Product Training
Strategies for Success

Copyright © 2009 Debra J. Smith

iUniverse books may be ordered through booksellers or by contacting:

iUniverse
1663 Liberty Drive
Bloomington, IN 47403
www.iuniverse.com
1-800-Authors (1-800-288-4677)

ISBN: 978-1-4401-2254-5 (pbk)
ISBN: 978-1-4401-2255-2 (ebk)

Library of Congress Control Number: 2009924782

Printed in the United States of America

iUniverse rev. date: 3/30/2009

This book is dedicated to my parents, who have always provided unconditional love and support. To my mom, who says I can make anything happen, and to my dad, who is famous for his words, "Don't memorize it—learn it!" They have been the guiding force in my life. I hope I have made them proud.

Contents

Acknowledgments

Many thanks to Victor Reddick who has guided me in my career and provided me with a wonderful opportunity. And of course thanks to my former team and good friends—Damian, Karen, Sue B., Sue H., Susan, John, Mary, Janet, and Chris—who helped keep me sane in GTE. I learned a lot from you during our time together. I want to express my heartfelt appreciation for all of your support—both personally and professionally. We had a good run, didn't we?

$Preface$

I have suffered through many tedious training lectures where I, along with scores of other people, just sat there and listened until my ears hurt, my eyes hurt, and … well, you get it. I thought to myself, "There must be a better way to train!" Having directed a learning organization, I found out firsthand how other employees like me just hated sitting through the endless hours of didactic lectures that are typically (and not so fondly) referred to as "death by PowerPoint."

After enrolling in a master's program in the field of education, I chose a topic for my action research project easily—implementing proven adult learning techniques that have been used in other educational centers. I wanted to use these methods to improve product training effectiveness in the medical device sales organization where I worked.

This book was written to help organizations improve learning retention and thus the success rate and confidence of employees when presenting product value to customers—particularly high-tech, complicated products. The implementation of innovative learning strategies in a common-sense approach to training contributes to an overall increase in employee and management satisfaction and in sales performance. Problem-based learning strategies are implemented to improve critical thinking skills in solving customer problems by presenting product features and benefits as solutions to those problems. Small learning groups are used to facilitate discussion and best practices. Solution selling is then best accomplished by thoroughly understanding and learning (not memorizing!) product features, functions, and benefits and by applying them to real-life customer situations.

This book is targeted at those companies selling products with advanced and/or complicated technologies, such as medical device companies. However, any product training department will benefit from the strategies outlined throughout this book.

Introduction

The goal of any product training is for attendees to be able to competently and confidently articulate product value to their customers, with the objective of a resulting product sale. This is especially true for salespeople; effectively presenting product features, functions, and benefits to a customer increases chances for a "win." The sales representative is responsible for initiating the conversation with a potential customer and increasing the interest that customer has in a company's products by effectively positioning the benefits that the product can offer. Customer benefits will be different depending on the market served. Each company employee has the responsibility of understanding product features and benefits. Effective positioning of the product is accomplished through the ability of the employee, such as a salesperson, to explain the value of the product features and benefits in a way that customers can understand and appreciate. The result is that the customer will more likely purchase that company's products and not a competitor's.

In the sales environment, salespeople deal with "objections" from the customer as a reason for the customer not buying their product (Gitomer 2006). Dealing with objections after the customer has vocalized them usually results in the loss of a sale. If the salesperson can proactively avoid getting objections from the customer, the likelihood of making a sale is higher. The only way to avoid customer objections proactively is to know in advance the customer's needs and how the product features can meet those needs. Knowing how product features can meet needs establishes trust with the customer, an important element in sales objectives (Campbell, Davis, and Skinner 2006). The ability of the salesperson to adapt the benefits of product features to the individual customer's needs positively affects trust and effectiveness of communication.

Sales representatives and other employees are required to attend new-hire and other product training courses, such as new product introductions and/ or upgrades (new features). The goal of a training department or training personnel is to present not only product information but also training strategies and tactics that ultimately result in increased competence of the salespeople (or any employees, for that matter) in their ability to effectively present that product to customers.

The training department is responsible for the development of the curriculum strategy and for implementing a paradigm shift in training, if so needed. The training staff creates the curriculum and is responsible for following that strategy. Each trainer maintains the curriculum for his or her classroom and meets regularly with other trainers to ensure that all the individual curriculum and materials for the training classes are consistent with the training strategy while meeting the needs of the students.

The problem is that employees may not receive adequate training to effectively present product features and benefits. Adequate training does not necessarily mean adequate content: many product training programs offer abundant and excellent product training material. The *way* that people are trained—that is, the strategic approach to behavioral modification—is as important as *what* people are trained on. Thus, a paradigm shift in training strategy may be indicated by introducing innovative learning techniques into the product training environment.

The following chapters outline the problem in more detail and provide a step-by-step solution to increase the effectiveness of product training programs.

Chapter 1 :

THE PROBLEM—THE CURRENT STATE OF PRODUCT TRAINING

Visualize a typical product training program: Large audiences. "Death by PowerPoint." Attendees sleeping, or worse, talking on cell phones. Managers leaving the room.

The problem is that product training classes usually consist of a "classic" lecture format with large audiences in auditorium-style settings. In most companies, product training classes are classic in design and do not consist of in-depth discussions on how each product feature and benefit can help solve customer problems. Most of the training time is spent defining the new product or feature. Few training hours are dedicated to discussion and practice on how customer benefits can be realized from the features of a product.

Conventional training consists of didactic lectures and handouts; PowerPoint presentations are the usual method of delivering information. Microphones are sometimes placed around the room in order to address questions from audience members. Most trainers and managers are comfortable with this classic approach and have used this one-way training style for years.

Most people are comfortable with the passive learning style that comes from conventional training techniques—it is how they learned in school.

After product training classes have finished, many companies find that their employees may be lacking in their ability to relate the learned product features to the benefits a customer would realize by buying the product (customer needs analysis). The lack in ability can be related to both confidence and competence in product value knowledge. For example, salespeople that learn product features may not retain the learned information—they have forgotten much of what they learned—as time passes after the training event. Their focus is shifted from remembering product benefits to each of their immediate problems of the day. Even if they understand how the product works, acting as consultants to their customers is virtually impossible unless the relation between product feature and benefit—and how that benefit can solve individual customer problems—is realized.

Many employees, such as sales representatives, and their managers are aware of this deficiency and may be dissatisfied with their level of skill presenting product features and benefits to customers. Worse yet, some may be totally unaware of their lack of skill level. In addition, most adults are dissatisfied and impatient with a passive learning format of training and desire a more interactive format. The result may be an overall lack of satisfaction with training and decreased confidence in selling and communicating to customers.

Many employees are bored with passive learning programs; the result is decreased satisfaction and attention.

In the sales environment, a number of causes exist that contribute to a salesperson's lack of competence in presenting product features and benefits to customers. One major cause may be an extremely young sales force if turnover of sales personnel is high. A sudden change of sales territories, commission structures, and other issues can result in a high dissatisfaction level and eventual turnover. Although some turnover is beneficial, such as in the termination of an underperforming salesperson, the loss of productive employees can be an expensive proposition. The result is a lack of experience in selling into the industry. New sales team members take time to become an expert consultant with their products. For example, some sales representatives are hired from companies that do not sell advanced technology. These sales representatives are familiar with the sales process but may not know how to relate the advanced product technology benefits to their new customers' needs. In general, sales team members that are more familiar with high-tech sales will have an advantage over those members that come from non-sales backgrounds or from selling lower technology and/or less complicated products.

One of the main causes of people failing to effectively present product value to potential customers is lack of adequate training techniques. Two main reasons exist for this ineffective training. The first reason is that the classic lecture format of product training is not effective for adequate learning; studies have shown that classic lecture format used in a typical product training session is unsuitable for adequate learning and does not create an effective learning environment. Product training at many companies consists of this classic lecture style; a large audience format is typical. The large audience style of classic lecture formats consists of passive learning and does not address different learning styles. Most instruction of this format directed at large groups of learners places heavy emphasis on lecturing on facts; thus instruction tends to relegate learners to a passive role in learning (Hunt, Haidet, Coverdale, and Richards 2002). As Raucent (2001) remarks, "There is a marked difference between what a teacher speaks about during a lecture and what students really absorb." Raucent goes on to state, "Students retain 10 percent of what they read, 26 percent of what they hear, 30 percent of what they see, 50 percent of what they see and hear, 70 percent of what they say, and 90 percent of what they say as they do something." Increased learning, therefore, is realized in a training model where the students are actively engaged in their own learning.

The lack of adequate training methodology can result in decreased effectiveness in presenting product value to customers.

The large audience format promotes a passive learning style and does not allow for interaction and case study and best practices sharing. Individual customer problems cannot be discussed in depth in an auditorium-type training setup. Few opportunities exist for including discussion sessions with the more experienced and successful sales representatives. The interest level in the large audience format of product training is extremely low.

The second reason that causes ineffective training is that classic training methods on product features lack real-world examples and case studies and many times focus more on drills and testing of the technology and feature definitions. Employees, such as sales representatives, thus will have inadequate experiential retention of learned material. For example, large volumes of advanced technological detail are typically presented to employees in a lecture session, but the vast amount of information precludes retentive learning. As described earlier, approximately 30 percent of the material is learned through visual presentation, which is the training format that dominates in these classic lecture sessions. In addition, the learned information is retained short-term only, because few sales team members ever review their "handout" material after the conclusion of training sessions. The product technology presented to the sales team members may be advanced; technical details are not understood by most of the students and only understood by those that have a similar product knowledge background.

The third reason for ineffective training is that no continued learning programs may exist to facilitate the retention and progression of learned information. Training in many circumstances is considered a one-time event, not a long-term process. Follow-up assignments for learning reinforcement are not mandated by many training departments. In addition, testing is not mandated at any training to assess the salesperson. Thus, no testing takes place to ensure that the students learn what they are supposed to learn. As a result, learning cannot be assumed.

Product training is a one-time event in most companies.

The last reason for ineffective training is the lack of accountability that the employees may have in their own learning. In many companies, no processes are put into place to demand that the employee know the new product or, more importantly, know the product benefits that translate to customer need fulfillment. Two reasons for this are that no assessments take place after training and the management may have a lack of confidence in the training itself. No action may be taken when employees, such as sales team members, demonstrate a lack of knowledge in competently presenting the product to customers. The action is taken long down the road when the salesperson fails. Most post-training documents that product trainers give to students are surveys to indicate participants' level of satisfaction with the training; this meets the bare minimum of a training evaluation and is beneficial for part of a summative evaluation, but it is not enough to assess whether the product training in totality was successful. Most learning organizations measure learning by following the Kirkpatrick Levels of Learning (appendix B). Kirkpatrick Level 1 is attained through surveys and measures how the attendees felt about the training. Obtaining Kirkpatrick Levels 2 (understanding how a product functions and learning benefits), 3 (application of that learning, both as a measure at the end of training and application in real-life situations), and sometimes even Level 4 (noticeable impact on the business) are necessary to prove product training success.

A positive post-training survey response does not indicate product training success by itself.

Chapter 2:
Adult Learning Theory

Adults desire to learn for several reasons. Some adults enroll in higher education programs and others either learn on the job or attend trade schools. For example, someone who wants to work as a mechanic either studies under an expert or attends mechanics' courses. If this does not happen, the young person will fail at his or her mechanical job and need to find other areas of employment. Motivation to hold a job and increase income thus becomes motivation to learn. This is the motivation of a typical corporate employee (such as a salesperson)—he or she needs to learn and master skills to be competitive in the global marketplace.

Current product training strategies parallel pedagogical learning, that is, education for children. Children are dependent learners and learn to achieve subsequent grade levels. Pedagogy features more passive learning, gathering, processing, and regurgitating of facts. Children rely on obtaining information from teachers and are expected to reflect on facts. However, even in pedagogical institutions, a paradigm shift in learning strategy is being adopted, incorporating more discovery learning principles.

Children, for the most part, are passive learners. Adults are not.

Andragogy is the science of educating adults. As most of us know, adults learn differently than children. Adults are volunteer learners and have a different motivation to learn. Much of how adults learn is based on experiences (experiential learning). Adults take what they learn and only retain the information that pertains to their experiential needs. Adults usually have a goal in mind when learning and take an active role in their education. Though adults learn facts throughout the learning process, they reflect on experiences, not facts as children do. Adults naturally are attracted to the learner-centered environment. However, most have probably had little previous experience in this type of learning environment.

Adults are volunteer learners and learn and retain information that pertains to their environment.

Thus, different learning strategies must be provided that focus on known andragogical practice. It is not only the delivery of content that is important but also knowing the processes that motivate adults to learn. Primary methods in pedagogy are passive in nature (e.g., assigned readings and lectures). Though reading assignments and lectures are a method for transferring information to adults, the next step in learning that is beneficial in andragogy is experiential in nature: case studies, discussion groups, and even gaming. Adults' reflection on their personal experiences mandate how strategies are incorporated into practical design and development of educational programs.

Standards exist for pedagogical learning (we all know about the No Child Left Behind Act of 2001). But no such standards exist for adult learning; expectations of learning outcomes can vary widely based on individual expectations and experience. This is especially true in the product training environment; most organizations, if standards are present at all, may not want to share best practices with competitors.

Motivation is a strong force in the formation of learning. Internal or external forces, personal drive, need for approval, and a desire for incentives or a sense of accomplishment, among others, can all demonstrate motivation. Motivators can be positive or negative. For example, a positive reinforcer would be a sale resulting from the student using appropriate learned sales mastery techniques. The motivating factor is the "win" incentive. Negative motivators exist as well. For example, if a student has been reprimanded for verbalizing, the chances of that student participating in discussion topics are reduced, due to the past punishment.

Second, the learning styles of adult students can influence areas of a curriculum. If the students' learning styles do not match the underlying social and cultural implications of the curriculum, learning may not be as effective or, in fact, may not take place. For example, a curriculum may stress social interaction over individual learning. Some students that learn best by working independently, or those needing special attention, may suffer. Collaborative projects that work well for some students may not work as well for others. Thus learning styles of adults need to be factored into the learning environment.

For adults, task-based learning is more important than memorization of content. Instruction that is focused on problem solving and that is pertinent to the adult's environment, concentrating on tasks such as case study examination, is suggested by many androgogical experts as a much more effective learning method. Discussion sessions where all students can express individual and unique experiences add to the richness of learning.

The "chunking" of information or informational sessions is as important as the information itself. Humans have a limit in the number of informational facts they can remember at one time. Chunking the information improves the student's ability to retain and comprehend the learning material. The more the information becomes highly technical (or complex), the less the amount of information presented for each discussion session. To implement chunking and realize its benefits, didactic and discussion segments need to be broken up into sequential but separate sessions. Enough time for discussion needs to be allowed, with frequent breaks between each session.

Four Keys to Adult Learning*

- Let adults direct themselves in the instructional process.

- Integrate new information with previous experiences.

- Make sure the information is relevant.

- Make sure the information is readily useable for the learner.

*From "Andragogy: Teaching Adults," *Encyclopedia of Education Technology,* August 19, 2007, http://coe.sdsu.edu/eet/Articles/andragogy/index.htm.

Chapter 3:
SMALL GROUP, PROBLEM-BASED LEARNING

The most appropriate strategy to train adults is one that is not passive and where students can apply their learning to real-life situations. Discussing cases with others and sharing experiences has much value. Therefore, increased learning is realized in a training model where the students are actively engaged in their own education. Increased effectiveness of learning can be seen in those classroom models where students are active learners and instructors are facilitators, rather than in the classical approach, where instructors tend to emulate the traditional model of lectures and the instructor is the center of attention (Vega and Tayler 2005). Raucent (2001) proposes moving from classical lectures to a problem-based learning approach, summed up as "learning by doing in small groups." Such studies point to evidence that small groups of students learn better by deeper student engagement and the ability for the teacher to incorporate multiple learning styles into this type of education.

Adults need to be actively engaged in their own learning.

The literature supports the idea that small group, problem-based learning techniques can increase the quality and retention of learned information. Large audience formats with passive learning styles have been replaced by small group, problem-based learning in regular schools and even medical schools, with positive learning results. Problem-based learning is used to enhance content knowledge and retention and is usually performed in small discussion teams with teachers acting as facilitators.

Small group, problem-based learning is a "best practice" approach for training adults.

The traditional content-focused, lecture-delivered instruction assesses student outcomes based on the quantity of information mastered. In traditional classrooms, students work alone and on assignments that demand short-term content memorization (Pearlman 2006). The students work for only the teacher and do not need to make presentations themselves. A shift has occurred toward adopting a problem-based learning approach that focuses on activity-based, student-centered learning that assesses student outcomes based on the ability to apply information and to develop critical-thinking skills to solve problems (Fenwick 2002). Traditional teaching approaches based on didactic and directive instruction have been replaced with the problem-based learning approach that fosters deeper learning (Fenwick 2002). Problem-based learning takes the approach that puts students into learning groups and introduces a problem that requires that the students work as a team to develop a plan of action to solve the problem. This method of learning enhances critical thinking, communication, and teamwork skills. Problem-based learning is not a new approach to education and has been practiced in educational institutions for approximately thirty years.

The higher quality of learning found during group interaction in problem-based learning can be explained in several ways. First, the discussions in learning groups "may have positive cognitive effects through reciprocal explanation, elaboration, and generation of learning issues" (Nieminen, Sauri and Lonka 2006). Secondly, commitment to learning may be enhanced by a group that functions well. Thirdly, the motivation of the student may be increased to invest in independent study time.

The inclusion of real or simulated problems is part of a problem-based learning environment and can result in the knowledge and attitudes necessary for one to make wise decisions on problems (Sungur, Tekkaya, and Geban 2006). Since there may be no right or wrong answer to a problem, the student in a problem-based learning classroom learns by seeking and developing skills to learn multiple solutions and apply the best solution to the problem. Problem-based learning can be effective in that various learning styles are addressed.

Also, problem-based learning helps students develop better critical thinking skills.

Problem-based learning enhances critical thinking skills, a skill highly valuable in the selling environment.

Dochy, Segers, Bossche, and Gijbels (2003) found in their meta-analysis that students in a problem-based learning environment "had slightly less knowledge, but remembered more of the acquired knowledge and applied it more effectively." The analysis shows that these students seem to remember more of the acquired knowledge because the learned information has been elaborated and studied in more depth.

The introduction of problem-based learning approaches shifts learning from a teacher-centered to a student-centered format. Increasing responsibility is placed on the student for his or her own learning (Sungur and Tekkaya 2006). As the learners are led through this process, they learn not to depend on teachers and instead become more independent learners throughout their education. This self-regulated learning has important implications to adult education. Sungur and Tekkaya (2006) have defined self-regulation as "the process that students use to activate and sustain their thoughts, behaviors, and emotions to reach their goals."

Problem-based learning teaches learners to ask questions, make observations, and test hypotheses to be able to thoroughly investigate a problem (Massaro, Harrison, and Soares 2006). The experiences in the problem-based learning environment build upon previous practical knowledge of the students.

According to Massaro, Harrison, and Soares, five basic steps to the problem-based learning process exist. The first is in encountering the problem. The second is identifying what is needed to learn within the learning group. The third is engaging in self-study. The fourth is applying the new knowledge to the problem in learning groups. The last is summarizing in the group what was learned.

Problem-based Learning in Andragogical Settings

Until recently, small group, problem-based learning has mostly been applied in academic settings. A substantial amount of research has been performed that has focused on "small group learning" and "problem-based learning" in andragogical educational settings, such as medical schools. Problem-based learning is used to enhance content knowledge and retention and is usually performed in small discussion teams with teachers or trainers acting as facilitators. Studies have shown that the small group setting is necessary for effective problem-based learning. These studies agree that the application of small group learning has a positive impact on the amount and quality of learning of the study subjects (De Villiers, Bresick, and Mash 2003). The conclusion supports the use of widespread implementation of small-group learning in undergraduate courses. Thus, problem-based learning incorporates shifting from training on "factual knowledge" to an active learning format with the addition of small learning groups.

Problem-based learning (PBL) is best implemented within small learning groups.

The small group structure in problem-based learning has been shown to develop a culture of both team learning and self-directed learning (Willis 2002). The results indicated that students "support PBL group work as a method of learning, and that those groups that work cooperatively are perceived as facilitating the most motivating learning environment." The students also found that they had more confidence when solving problems individually after their experience in the small learning groups.

Problem-based Learning in the Product Training Environment.

Problem-based learning has not been introduced into mainstream corporate training until very recently. Few research studies have been documented that demonstrate the value of evaluating the small group, problem-based learning approach in the corporate training environment, especially in product training. Unofficial reports of integrating problem-based learning techniques in the sales environment have been described through the formation of small groups of salespeople who trained through the case-study approach and through interaction with other salespeople. Few additional articles were available on this subject until the first few years of the twenty-first century. As Fenwick (2002) states, "Few programs employ problem-based learning in graduate education, and little research focuses on the mid-career professionals and problem-based learning." Though more articles can be found every day that deal with problem-based learning in corporate (HR) training or even sales mastery programs, few articles have been uncovered that examine the role of problem-based learning in the product training environment.

Problem-based learning uses a case-study approach to provide the employees with a way to discuss current customer situations and think critically about solutions based on learned product features and benefits. In the problem-based learning environment, students are provided problems that require them to define multiple causes for that problem, develop several solutions, and then justify those solutions according to critical thinking. Problems are presented more effectively in the guise of case studies. "Case studies are one of the most dynamic methods to beckon learners down their own pathways of learning" (Santanello and Hilebrandt 2005). The case study approach to product training will ensure that the student can relate product features and benefits to customers. For example, in the sales environment, customers will "buy confidence." Raymond (2006) states, "[Customers] choose the salesperson who can best convince them that he can solve their problems." Adult learners, such as salespeople, seem to be more motivated to learn when they can use the learned information in these real-life situations (Brewer, Klein, and Mann 2003). In the earlier discussion of self-regulation, these skills are of little value if students do not motivate themselves to use them (Sungar and Tekkaya 2006). Part of the self-motivation belief forms a basis for self-efficacy theory, which refers to the student's belief about his or her own ability to perform effectively. The use of learning groups facilitates self-learning and self-confidence (self-efficacy) as demonstrated in research by Willis (2002). The value of self-efficacy of sales team members cannot be understated as they attempt to gain the trust and confidence of their customers. The small group, problem-based learning approach would allow sales teams to learn information in a way that would prepare them to be more effective in presenting product features and benefits to customers.

Problem-based learning in the sales environment uses a real-life, case study approach to stimulate experiential learning.

In order to be able to answer customers' questions about products, companies need to find more innovative ways like problem-based learning to train their employees. For example, problem-based training methods are vital in effectively selling into markets such as healthcare. According to Webster (2006), "Most companies are adept at dispensing the information that the physicians need. They can put together data that sales people require to adequately know their product." However, salespeople need to relate the data to the customer in a way that solves the customer' problems (and that the customer can understand!). Learning to relate to customer needs in this way has been a problem in sales and product training for a long time.

Small group, problem-based learning has been recently introduced as an effective product training technique. The introduction of problem-based learning demonstrates an andragogical shift from traditional content-focused, lecture-delivered instruction that focused on quantity of information toward more activity-based, student-centered learning that creates the ability for a student to apply information and think critically about solutions (Fenwick 2002). Small group learning develops students' problem-solving skills, which is beneficial in many areas of life (Crosby 2004), and allows the student to achieve a deeper understanding of the topic in order to challenge assumptions.

Hall (2005) surveyed sales organizations to investigate sales training issues; most of those sales organizations communicated significant problems with the old style of classroom-based training. The issues included high costs with perceived low return and the lack of transfer of what the salespeople had learned to the workplace. All agreed that face-to-face instruction was needed, but the training method needed to be more effective and better meet the needs of the sales force.

Though this book focuses on product training strategies, small group, problem-based learning can be applied to the subject matter of any presentation, and the elements can result in better retention of the presenter's message and material (Kasuya 2004). As Kasuya states, "The challenge is to transform a lecture hall into an environment where each attendee is actively participating in his or her own learning and actively contributing to the overall education of the group." Even presentations at conventions can benefit by a paradigm shift in the way the audience members participate in the lecture.

The key features approach to problem-based learning is based on the assumption that only a few essential elements that provide the necessary steps to solve a problem exist (Farmer and Page 2005). Key features are unique to each problem; constructing the component features results in a better workup and management of the problem. This approach may be useful when assessing skills that students acquire in a problem-based learning environment.

The application of small group, problem-based learning tactics has been applied mostly to the face-to-face classroom setting. In product training, face-to-face sessions may happen infrequently. In order to facilitate long-term knowledge and retention of learned material, continual education and reinforcement is crucial for success. Classroom and computer-based training (CBT) can provide multiple mechanisms for delivery of educational information and continued learning. Small group, problem-based learning techniques can be applied both in the classroom and in CBT.

Problem-based learning using small learning groups can be implemented within the blended learning environment.

In addition, problem-based learning is best performed in small learning groups (Albanese 2001). Problem-based learning usually uses case studies to solve real-life problems. This constructivist method requires that students work together in small groups to acquire the knowledge and skills needed for professional practice (Arts, Gijselaers, and Segers 2006). The workplace requires that the case studies used in the small learning groups are realistic and consist of "real-world" problems. The potential of small group learning is greatly enhanced by this addition of the problem-based learning methods. The construction of the learning groups is vital for success.

In order for a learning group to function successfully, each member must be committed to collaboration. Any effective team melds together each individual's ideas and works toward a common goal, embracing each team member's strengths and weaknesses. Collaboration is essential to the team's performance and completion of the desired task. All the strengths of each member have to be pulled together when developing teams. One member may have a wealth of knowledge in using different sales skills, another may be an excellent problem solver, and another member may have superior verbal and written communication skills. These strengths can be combined to form a successful learning group. However, learning groups are not always effective and can bring out the worst in people if not formed properly. To be effective, the team size should be small and have a diversity of people, this providing a variety of skills and ideas to encompass the group. The group should not be composed of mostly dominating team members who may push their ideas onto the group, resulting in decreased learning for the other team members. The leadership should be shared among all team members, although there must be someone who will assume responsibility for pulling those ideas together. Collaboration not only provides much needed synergy within a team and adds to a company's success, it also enhances the individual's ability to expand his or her knowledge on a particular subject. Collaboration assists in giving an idea multiple facets with the input from team members and their knowledge on the subject matter.

> Success of product training using small group, problem-based learning methods is dependent upon the interaction within the learning group.

The success of problem-based learning in the product training environment lies with the facilitator, the implementation of curriculum, the small learning groups, and the use of technology for continued learning.

The implementation of problem-based learning techniques into the product training classes increases the competence and confidence of employees in communicating product features and benefits to customers in a way to which customers can relate.

The use of problem-based learning strategies in the sales training environment are an effective way to increase the level of skill sales representatives have in presenting product features and benefits to customers. Sales training can implement the problem-based learning approach by using a case study strategy involving real-life customer situations. Critical thinking skills are enhanced, especially for the new sales representative, by using this form of learning.

The first way that the small group format enhances learning is that the students can discuss various customer problem scenarios and share possible solutions in a non-threatening environment. Using a team-based approach, a customer problem, in the form of a case study, is provided to each learning group, and the learning group has to decide collectively the best way to solve the problem. The participation and the learning is active and much better accepted than the traditional classroom approach. A facilitator should be appointed to each learning group to keep the discussions on track.

The second way the small group format enhances the learning experience is through the actual construction of the learning groups. Teaming veterans with inexperienced employees is of a value that cannot be understated. Case studies that are used within the discussion groups are based on real-life customer situations and are gathered by the trainers through experienced employees. During the customer case study situation, the inexperienced student draws on the knowledge of the more experienced student and is therefore able to grow his or her knowledge of what does and what does not work in presenting product features and benefits to customers.

Some employees, such as sales representatives, may have been hired away from competitive companies. The third way that the small learning groups enhanced learning is through incorporating those who have in-depth knowledge of the competition into each learning group. By active participation in the group, the employee hired from another competitor has valuable information to provide the group, whether he or she is inexperienced or experienced.

In conclusion, the implication of the outcomes is clear. The implementation of problem-based learning strategies is important to the overall effectiveness of every employee. The format of the product training sessions needs to include small discussion groups where real-life customer case studies can be used as training examples.

Chapter 4:

THE FIVE PHASE PLAN: A BLENDED LEARNING APPROACH

Product training is not and should not be a one-time event. A phased approach to product training is suggested by this author to ensure success of learning and to provide a means to measure that success. The Five Phase Plan consists of pre-training surveys and assessments to formulate a student baseline, pre-work assignments prior to a training event, a face-to-face training event, post-training surveys and assessments, and continuing education programs. The small group, problem-based learning approach can be implemented in many of the phases of product training. The curriculum that is developed throughout the Five Phase approach should be guided by a widely used principle of instructional systems design such as the ADDIE model. Appendix A provides more information on this instructional systems design model.

The Five Phase Plan is a blended learning approach. Blended learning means that a combination of classroom and computer- or Web-based training (CBT or WBT) is used to facilitate learning retention. Singh and Reed (2001) define blended learning as "a learning program where more than one delivery mode is being used, with the objective of optimizing the learning outcome and cost of program delivery."

Understanding the benefits of using blended learning in product training will assist the reader in better understanding and implementing the Five Phase Plan into his or her learning institution.

Many benefits exist in using the blended learning approach, and thus in using the Five Phase Plan, for product training. The time taken to bring people together to launch and train employees on new products can be dramatically decreased. Much of the product training content can be delivered via the Web, with less (but higher quality) time spent in the classroom. Learners can access expertise at any time through the use of technology. Training content can be reviewed at the learner's convenience via CBT or WBT. Blended learning provides a continuous learning process—not the traditional "one-shot" approach so often seen in product training programs. Since training should never be a single event, blended learning offers the best of both worlds: training that is both "face to face" and "anytime you need it." Most face-to-face events are found in the classroom; other training programs can be efficiently deployed via WBT or CBT.

Current classroom training is more social and provides the opportunity for face-to-face interactions and discussions. Classroom training can be a more structured approach for some individual students, and the instructor can more readily apply one-on-one instruction. The instructor is closer to the students and can assess not only their progress but also their attitude and motivation. Motivation of the adult learner is important in learning, as discussed in chapter 2.

A tremendous strength of WBT is the ability of the program to reach multiple learning styles just like classroom-based experiences. Web-based training provides targeted "when-you-need-it" training and training updates for reinforcement of material already learned. Web-based training can also be more economical, as little or no travel time and costs are ensued. Web-based training can be instructor-led or self-study and offers an interactive way to present learning over the Web. This distance delivery system is suited for employees all over the world. Since these programs contain various delivery technologies, multiple learning styles are addressed. Presentations with multimedia appeal to visual learners. Audio recordings with the presentation address auditory learners. Chat sessions partially address kinesthetic learners. If needed, the online presentation/lecture can be printed out for those kinesthetic learners needing more support.

Web-based programs can be instructor-led or self-paced.

Web-based programs can be used very effectively for real-time training programs. For example, one could provide a live training program on a new technology. The program includes a presentation using multimedia to demonstrate technical points and audio of the speaker giving the presentation. The incorporation of multimedia with PowerPoint is the cornerstone of most training programs. The lecturer is heard (or even seen) presenting the lecture and a simultaneous chat room session can be available to take questions throughout the presentation. The live chat room is provided so that participants can type in questions throughout the program. More companies are deploying blogging and chat rooms within their secure training Web sites. Chat rooms are a great way to tap into the knowledge of top performers without significantly decreasing their productivity.

Another strength is the flexibility of WBT to offer archived presentations. The entire program, including the presentation, audio, and chat questions, can be archived so that those people unable to attend the training can take the program at a later date. The chat room can be reactivated so that experts from other areas of the world are able to participate. Those students unavailable for the real-time presentation can review the archived study, the only drawback of which is the lack of real-time interaction. However, the archived presentation can be presented in a quasi-live format. For example, the presentation can be played from the archive with a local expert at the training site as facilitator. The archived lecture could potentially be played to a group with an expert on hand to answer questions.

The last strength is that WBT offers program, assessment, and evaluation within (usually) one software program. Instant polling is available, as well as post-test assessments and tracking.

One weakness with WBT includes bandwidth limitations of the Internet within different countries. Those students who have slow Internet connections may find the quality of the program decreased from those students with faster Internet connections. However, any bandwidth issues are related more to the Internet in general, and in some cases to the company's firewall, than to anything specific to the WBT program.

Bandwidth can limit the level of interactivity and multimedia used in a training program.

A second weakness stems from the inherent setup in the program, where a drop in the program signal can occur randomly, though reconnection usually is automatic. Thirdly, the use of extensive multimedia in a presenter's

PowerPoint presentation will slow down the program. In some cases, the audio lags and has to catch up with the video.

The blended learning approach in product training is discussed in an article by Hall (2005), in which several of the nation's top sales training organizations were surveyed to uncover "best practices" in sales training. Small group format using face-to-face training, combined with e-learning technologies, provided the best quality of learning for the sales representatives.

Let us now understand the components of each phase of the Five Phase Plan in developing a new product training curriculum.

$Phase\ I$ —

BASELINE ASSESSMENTS AND SURVEYS

Assessments

In any strategic plan, one must know where one currently is to determine the steps to where one wants to go in the future. In order to track learning progress, assessment of all students on current product knowledge is a necessary baseline activity. The assessment provides valuable information to stage each student's competence and confidence with discussing current product features and benefits with customers. Proving training effectiveness and outcomes, discussed in chapter 6, necessitates the completion of baseline assessments.

Using baseline assessments will help stage each student and facilitate individual action plans.

Ideally, two training or employee managers assess each employee on his or her competency in presenting product value to customers. This assessment usually takes place at regional or local meetings but could be performed centrally or prior to a product training event. It is recommended that managers should not assess their own employees due to bias complications. The four major categories needed to adequately score the employee consist of competency in describing product features and technology, communication of product benefits, relating features and benefits to those customer needs, and knowledge of competition. Each category is scored from 1 to 4, with a 4 being "excellent" and 1 being "poor." The highest total that could be obtained is 20. The assessment of each employee is based on the total score obtained. An assessment score of 15 and over is considered a passing score. An assessment score below 15 is considered a failing score. Those receiving failing scores should retake new-hire product training programs. Sample content in a rubric of such an assessment is shown below.

Table 1. Baseline Assessment Rubric

CATEGORY	4	3	2	1	Score
Product features and function	Shows a full understanding of the topic.	Shows a good understanding of the topic.	Shows a good understanding of parts of the topic.	Does not seem to understand the topic very well.	
Product feature benefits	Student is able to accurately answer almost all questions posed by instructor about the topic.	Student is able to accurately answer most questions posed by instructor about the topic.	Student is able to accurately answer a few questions posed by instructor about the topic.	Student is unable to accurately answer questions posed by instructor about the topic.	
Relating benefits to customer needs	Student is completely prepared and has obviously rehearsed.	Student seems pretty prepared but might have needed a couple more rehearsals.	The student is somewhat prepared, but it is clear that rehearsal was lacking.	Student does not seem at all prepared to present.	
Demonstrates knowledge of competition	Student is able to state three reasons why X company is better than the competition clearly and concisely.	Student is able to state clearly and concisely at least two reasons why X company is better than the competition.	Student is able to state two reasons why X company is better than competition but is somewhat unclear.	Student is able to state only one reason why X company is better than competition and is not clear in this description.	
Case study	Excellent correlation of product benefits to customer problem	Good correlation of product benefits to customer problem	Some correlation of product benefits to customer problem; needs work	No correlation of product benefit to customer problem; confused	

New employees, especially salespeople, should be exempt from this field activity until at least six months into the job, but they should have assessments at the conclusion of their new-hire product training sessions to provide a baseline.

A Word or Two about Assessments

Performance-based assessment is the current "best practice." This type of assessment has many advantages over other types. One advantage is that performance-based assessments may have a motivational benefit because they seem more relevant to real-world experiences. Another advantage is that the assessments can be complex and students tend to continue to learn throughout each assessment (Taylor and Nolan 2005). Performance-based assessments include a set of rules for what is expected of the student. This set of rules can more commonly be seen in the form of a rubric, as demonstrated in Table 1. Current best practice dictates that the performance "rules" match the learning goals and objectives (Taylor and Nolan 2005, pg. 84). Though content knowledge needs to be assessed, knowledge of content can be tested while critical thinking skills are enhanced through the use of performance-based assessments.

Performance-based assessment is accomplished two ways, both of which complement one another. The first way is by assessing all students at the same time through formal classroom testing. Another way is to assess the student individually. Individual assessment can provide the opportunity to uncover specific areas of a student's skills and a need for additional instruction. For example, primary-level teachers will have students read aloud to uncover their comprehension level (Taylor and Nolan 2005).

In business school, new standards indicate the importance of assessing student learning and using the assessment data obtained to improve curriculum (Martell 2007). Current research points to the movement away from multiple choice and "one answer" student assessment strategies to those that involve more critical thinking skills. The use of assessments that ask students to perform tasks that are more complex and concrete is more often the norm (Shavelson 2007). Knowledge of content is important but more so is complex problem solving and analytical reasoning. The use of "performance" tasks that mimic real-life situations is used more often. For example, in business school a student may be asked to solve a problem after being given multiple sources of information, some of which are relevant and some that are not. The student then needs to analyze the information provided to determine a realistic solution. The task can be in the form of a business memo or PowerPoint presentation. The student then presents the information in a way so as to recommend the solution to a hypothetical board of directors. The student's performance is scored with the recognition that alternative solutions are possible (Shavelson 2007).

In the product training classroom, the students are assessed in two ways. One is content-based learning, where the students are tested on the concrete information they have learned. For example, part of new-hire product training involves lectures on product features and technology. The features, functions, and benefits of the product are presented in lecture format, either via WBT or in a classroom. The students are given a test to ensure that they are able to comprehend the features and other attributes of the product in order to increase their product knowledge. The students are required to know the basic product descriptions and have written tests that assess their knowledge.

Another type of assessment is performance-based. The students are given an oral examination to ensure that they are able to comprehend the benefits and other attributes of the product in order to effectively communicate product value to a customer. The learners are given a real-life customer case study where they have to think about what the solution would be for a customer, given a few facts about the case study. Though various scenarios can play out, the solution involves correctly pairing the system feature with the benefit the customer would realize in buying that company's products. A panel of trainers assesses each scenario and provides scores for each learner on a rubric. The rubric consists of elements directly relating to the goals and objectives of the training program. The rubric scores are added and the results reported to the learner's direct manager and kept in the training record files.

Care should be taken in developing the assessment. Content-based testing should address Kirkpatrick Level 2 of learning (knowledge). The performance-based assessment should address Kirkpatrick Level 3 of learning (transfer). Appendix B provides more on the Kirkpatrick levels.

Surveys

A survey of students and managers should also be undertaken as a baseline. The purpose of the survey is to uncover the student's level of personal confidence in communicating product features and value. The survey will also provide the level of the student's satisfaction with the delivery of the training programs. All managers should participate in the survey and should be copied on their employee's results, both from the survey and from the assessment. All stakeholders should receive the overall results from the surveys and the assessments. The survey and a letter of introduction to survey participants can be found below.

Example 1. Letter of Survey Introduction

To all students:

Attached is a link to a survey to assess the quality of product training sessions.

The purpose of this survey is to seek information on the quality of the product training from your perspective and from that of your manager. To complete the survey, simply check the answer that seems to be most relevant for you. All information you provide will remain completely confidential.

Please complete the survey within two weeks. One name from the respondent list will be randomly chosen to win a Blackberry!

Only with your feedback can we continue to enhance our training sessions. Thank you for taking the time to share your thoughts with us.

Best regards,

Table 2. Pre-training Survey

Sample: Student Survey

The following is a survey to seek information about the quality of previous product training from your perspective and that of your manager. To complete the survey, highlight the answer that seems to be most relevant for you.

Name: _____

1. The size of the class facilitated learning and discussion.

Strongly agree   Agree   Neither agree/disagree   Disagree Strongly disagree

2. There was ample opportunity for "hands-on" time.

Strongly agree   Agree   Neither agree/disagree   Disagree Strongly disagree

3. I learned the new technologies in a way that I easily related back to the customer.

Strongly agree   Agree   Neither agree/disagree   Disagree Strongly disagree

4. There was ample opportunity to learn and discuss the positioning of each new product feature.

Strongly agree   Agree   Neither agree/disagree   Disagree Strongly disagree

5. There was adequate time for team discussion.

Strongly agree   Agree   Neither agree/disagree   Disagree Strongly disagree

6. Real-life customer situations were addressed with this training.

Strongly agree   Agree   Neither agree/disagree   Disagree Strongly disagree

7. After training I felt confident to competently present product feature, functions, and benefits.

Strongly agree   Agree   Neither agree/disagree   Disagree Strongly disagree

8. After training I confidently and competently explained the new features and presented the product effortlessly to customers.

Strongly agree   Agree   Neither agree/disagree   Disagree Strongly disagree

9. The training positively impacted sales numbers.

Strongly agree   Agree   Neither agree/disagree   Disagree Strongly disagree

10. I was satisfied with the training and its format.

Strongly agree   Agree   Neither agree/disagree   Disagree Strongly disagree

Comments:_____

_____

_____

_____

Table 3. Survey Results Compilation Table Example

Survey Population (Student/ Managers)	Survey Results			
Scale	Strongly Disagree	Disagree	Agree	Strongly Agree
1. The size of the training class facilitated learning and discussion.				
2. There was ample opportunity for hands-on time.				
3. I learned the new technologies in a way that I easily related back to the customer.				
4. I had ample opportunity to learn and discuss the positioning of the new product features.				

5. There was adequate time for team discussion.				
6. Real-life customer situations were addressed with this training.				
7. After training, I confidently and competently explained the new features and presented the product effortlessly to customers.				
8. After training, I felt confident to position the product upgrade to my customers in a way they can relate to.				
9. The training positively impacted sales numbers.				
10. I was satisfied with the training and its format.				

A Word or Two about Surveys

Surveys can easily be performed in the online environment. If the company does not have a learning services Web site, the training manager can set up an account via online survey services, such as Zoomerang˚ (www.zoomerang. com). Most people have access to the World Wide Web, and online surveys are more easily tabulated and tracked than hardcopy or e-mailed surveys. However, hardcopy surveys can be mailed to participants and mailed back to the trainer using a self-addressed stamped envelope. This is made more difficult in a global environment, so the online approach is strongly suggested. Another alternative is to use e-mail as a survey delivery vehicle. Forms can be attached to the e-mail, filled out, and e-mailed back. Keep in mind that, although a valuable source of information, surveys address only the Kirkpatrick Level 1 of learning and are not appropriate as an indication that actual learning has taken place or as a measure of training success.

Surveys are more easily documented and tracked using the online environment.

Results from employees and management should be kept separate. Comparisons between the two can prove to provide valuable information and insights. More about this comparison is discussed in chapter 6.

Both assessments and surveys should be considered mandatory. The assessments, being face-to-face action, are more controllable. Completion of surveys should be carefully monitored, and messages from management reinforcing the need for compliance should be part of the survey introductory letter. Another way to ensure better compliance is to hold a prize drawing from those names submitting surveys.

Phase II —

PRE-WORK

To facilitate the classroom-based learning experience, homework should be provided to the students before the main training event to increase familiarity with the new product or upgrade and its features and technology. Two benefits arise from this strategy. The first is that the more familiar the student is with the product description, the more the training can focus on applying product feature benefits to real-life customer needs, thus providing a richer and more substantial training program. The second is that the longer students have to sit through a long, detailed product description lecture, the more likely the students will lose interest and attention; thus learning retention will be significantly reduced.

Pre-training assignments will enhance the product training experience.

Pre-training homework can be accomplished in several ways. The first way is through computer-based training methods (CBT). A CD or DVD using a multimedia presentation format can be sent to each student and used for a tutorial on the product technology and features. The advantage to this type of training is that is a self-study program and the student can "attend" whenever he or she has the time and wherever the student wishes without the need to connect to the Internet. The student can also review the tutorial, or sections of the tutorial, as many times as needed to retain the information. The disadvantage to this type of training is that the distribution of material is not under tight competitive control. That is, anyone could obtain the DVD and view the contents. This could be potentially devastating with new product introductions. Thus, security measures need to be put in place that would require the student to enter a code to view the training program. Another disadvantage is that distribution can be a huge problem as the number of students increase and the reach is global.

Distribution issues may prohibit the use of DVD programs as a vehicle for training delivery.

Tutorials can be placed on an internal training Web site and can sometimes be downloaded to individual computers. This is a more secure way of viewing product training presentations and is more convenient for some students, particularly if the training is to be globally focused. Most companies have an LMS (Learning Management System) and technical help for incorporating Web-based training methods. Those that do not have an LMS should consider the investment; not only does the LMS offer capability for Web-based training, but assessments and surveys can also be kept on file and easily viewed and tracked for each student. Trends in learning can be readily identified, for individuals as well as groups.

The Web is a great vehicle to deliver both self-paced and real-time training programs. Product training lectures are easily accomplished via live Web programs (webinars). For example, one could provide a live training program on a new technology or feature. The presentation includes a PowerPoint presentation with multimedia to demonstrate technical points and audio of the speaker giving the presentation. A live chat room is provided and participants can type in technical questions throughout the program. The live programs, including the written chat room questions and answers can be archived for those unable to attend the live session or for those students needing a review of the material. In addition, the archived presentation can be presented in a quasi-live format. For example, the presentation can be played from the archive with a local expert at the training site as facilitator. The chat room can be reactivated so that experts from other areas of the world participate. The advantage to this type of program is that it can be more interactive, as live chat sessions provide an opportunity for the students to ask questions from the product experts. An alternative to the online chat sessions is to provide a simultaneous teleconference. For some learners this approach may be preferable; however, with international attendance and those whose native language is different from the presenter, the chat room format works best. Chunking the information, as discussed in chapter 2, is easily accomplished in this type of Web environment. A series of presentations creates the total product technology lecture and is viewed by the learner at his or her convenience.

The Internet is a great way to deliver both instructor-led and self-paced training programs.

For both Web-based programs, security is generally assured since the student needs to provide his or her employee number and a pass code provided by the training department or LMS. In addition, a roster of attendees helps to assure compliance with program attendance.

Online testing after program attendance is essential to determine the level of product knowledge and learning retention. Test questions should address the Kirkpatrick Level 2 level of learning (appendix B). Those students failing to pass should retake the product technology/feature tutorials and retake the test. Attending the main training event is based on a passing score on the online test. This may seem harsh but face-to-face training is expensive and the pre-work understanding is important to reach the objectives of the classroom training event. Also, the student has the ability to take the test multiple times to pass. Compliance with program attendance and individual test scores is sent to the students' supervisors immediately upon compilation.

Testing is vital to check on attainment of knowledge.

In some circumstances, marketing and sales management may want to keep product introductions as a surprise to both the students and especially the competition. If the consensus is to accomplish all training at the main event, time needs to be added to the training program, significantly impacting the cost of the product launch event and reducing the time for the student's personal productivity or the time a salesperson has selling in the field. Not only will this add time to the face-to-face training event, but it may also impact learning productivity of the students. Too much information provided to the students in too little time will reduce learning retention and thus the effectiveness of the training program.

Maintaining an element of surprise for a new product may mandate alternative strategies for pre-training assignments.

Another option that could be considered is to still have pre-work for the students but keep it basic and provide the needed detailed information immediately prior to the training event. To make the students sign non-disclosures before they take the tutorial could increase attention and make the product launch seem more mysterious and exciting. Even if word starts to leak out to competition and the general public, the momentum of the product or upgrade introduction and launch could start earlier and inherently be greater. In fact, some marketing organizations prefer to intentionally "leak" word of a product launch for just that reason.

Phase III —
THE MAIN TRAINING EVENT

The third phase of product training is the implementation of the face-to-face main training event. A paradigm shift occurs in training strategy and tactics using the Five Phase approach. The classical large audience format of training is replaced with smaller learning groups to facilitate the advantages of problem-based learning techniques and includes small group or learning team discussions of real-life customer problems. Problem-based learning is implemented to include case studies and real-life customer situations. Both experienced as well as inexperienced employees are asked before the training commences to submit their own case studies of customer experiences, both successful and unsuccessful. Discussion groups are formed and consist of small groups using the problem-based learning approach. The learning groups consist of no more than eight students at a learning station. For example, in a typical product training venue such as a hotel ballroom, there are learning stations positioned throughout the room. Each learning station has a sample product for demonstration purposes.

The composition of learning groups consists, where feasible, of members from the same functional group. In the case of salespeople, the learning groups contain people from the same sales region or territory. Each sales territory is disaggregated so that experienced sales team members (those with more than two years of experience) are teamed with inexperienced members (those with less than two years of experience). This ensures that modeling can take place for a richer learning experience, increased self-efficacy of each team member, and enhancement of each team member's confidence. Self-efficacy is also important in increasing learning in group dynamics and characteristics. For more on modeling and self-efficacy in learning, see appendix C.

Training events use small group, problem-based learning strategies to provide a richer learning experience.

The curriculum consists of brief didactic lectures followed by a brief product demonstration and presentation of real-life customer problems. The lecture segments introduce the new product feature with emphasis on the benefits that a customer may realize from acquiring those features. The lectures are "chunked" into areas representing main product technology and features. Each lecture segment is immediately followed by discussion group activity.

The new product with its features and technology is also available and demonstrated in each learning group area. After each lecture segment, the product expert provides a demonstration of the product feature/technology and reinforces the benefits provided by the feature. The product expert is usually a facilitator and can lead the group discussions that follow the product demonstration.

The learning group agenda consists of the facilitator presenting the members with a problem chosen from submitted case studies and/or customer situations. The purpose of the learning group is to come up with a solution for the customer case study based on the product features and benefits learned during the tutorials and classroom discussions. Each of the learning group members has a specified amount of time to independently think about the situation. The learning group then gathers together and takes the proposed solution thought of by each learning team member and constructs a group solution using what the majority brainstormed as the best combination of all solutions presented. The learning group then chooses a representative to present their solution to the entire training audience. Discussion of all groups follows and microphones are made available at each learning station to facilitate discussion. In some cases, additional training value would be achieved if actual customers were present to determine if the proposed solutions would meet their needs. The customer's needs should match those submitted earlier by the learning group members to ensure validity of the discussions. Luminary customers are partners with the company and are usually receptive to helping in product training situations—particularly if the luminaries helped to develop the product features or technology.

Learning groups address customer problems by applying benefits to product features in the form of a customer solution.

Newly introduced material presented during product training consists of only the vital "take-away" information. Product feature or technology details should be handed out as reference material only for the sales team members to take home and use as needed. A note on handouts: placing presentations and product feature/technology details on a DVD is more advisable than large notebooks; much of the time the student does not want to pack a large notebook in a suitcase and will leave the material in his or her hotel room. In discussions and surveys with students in the past, a DVD is favored over a large product training book. A simple, small blank notebook for writing notes as necessary is preferable. In addition, a simple workbook consisting of sections following the training agenda and including the discussion group topics can assist each learning team member in documenting his or her thoughts as to customer solutions. Each section mimics what is typically known as "think sheets" in the learning world.

Don't make huge product training binders—for the most part they will just be ignored and thrown away.

Facilitation of the Learning Group

Problem-based learning is a dynamic process where tight interaction of the learning group, curriculum, and facilitator is needed for success. The role of the facilitator is to help the learning group approach big concepts in the case study, identify open-ended questions that encourage group discussion, and help the group identify their learning needs. Facilitators of the learning groups keep the group focused on the task at hand and act as a guide to enable critical thinking about the problem and potential solutions. Facilitators should take care not to dominate group discussion and provide ready answers when the group appears to be "stuck." The facilitator needs at times to ask open-ended questions and act more as a coach to help expand discussion and foster group-centered learning. The group facilitators are comprised of training managers and/or those who have already been trained in the facilitating of group discussion. Product experts are an important partner with the training managers. Training classes on facilitation should be offered in the months prior to the main product feature training. Facilitators should be required to pass an aptitude test demonstrating that they are competent at facilitating group discussion. Facilitator training is not a long, painful process and should be looked upon as an opportunity to learn.

Facilitators act as guides to helping learning groups focus on the customer problem and to find solutions.

A meeting should be held between the training department and the managers of the attendees immediately after the training event. Discussions that should take place include what went well with the training format and what could be improved. Notes taken on this discussion are sent out to all participating in the meeting. Suggested changes can be implemented in the next face-to-face training session if deemed appropriate by the training department.

Phase IV—
Post-training Assessments and Surveys

Testing

Content-based testing should take place throughout product training to ensure that participants reach a basic knowledge level of the product and its features and benefits. This can take the form of quizzes and be formal or informal. The intent is to ensure Kirkpatrick Level 2 has been achieved. Otherwise the next level—the application of learning to solve customer problems—will probably not occur.

Assessments

The last section of product training consists of assessments of the learning team members' ability to competently (and confidently!) present product features (technology), functions, and benefits in a way that provides solutions to customer problems. The assessment format is almost identical to that completed prior to the training event with the exception that the assessment is performed within each learning group. Individual students within each learning team need to articulate product features, functions, and benefits, as well as compare them to competition. Each student presents in front of the other learning group members as the facilitator assesses his or her performance. More experienced team members should start, with less experienced members presenting last. The reason for this format is that the students learn and build on each other's thoughts. Thus, more learning takes place during the assessments. The students, particularly those who are newer to the organization, may feel uncomfortable in presenting in front of their peers; however, this practice will be valuable when presenting in front of an actual customer.

Performance assessments take place within learning groups.

The last part of each individual assessment should include a case study of a real customer problem. The case studies presented during the brief lectures make ideal topics during the testing. The solutions presented by the student should include the product features and how the benefits will help solve the customer problem. Since the topics are chosen from discussions ensuing from the main training session, the students should have had plenty of time to acquire the knowledge needed to competently present.

The assessments should be performed by training managers and learning group facilitators, depending on the number of students in the training event. In some instances, the attendees' managers desire to be involved in the assessments. If these managers do assist in the assessments, they should not assess their own subordinates. Bias in scoring is less likely if the assessor does not know the student. In addition, the managers of the attendees should attend meetings on assessment skills facilitation. Using more than one assessor is advisable if at all possible.

The rubric for scoring is identical to that used in the baseline assessment (see table 1.) The assessor should not only provide the numerical data in the rubric but also detailed notes on the student's presentation style, attitude, and other factors that may impact his or her ability to effectively present product value to customers. An example of a completed assessment is shown below.

Table 4. Example of a Completed Assessment for a Salesperson

Name: John Smith   Years with company: 3   Region: Southwest

CATEGORY	4	3	2	1	Score
Product features and function	Shows a full understanding of the topic.	Shows a good understanding of the topic.	Shows a good understanding of parts of the topic.	Does not seem to understand the topic very well.	4
Product feature benefits	Student is able to accurately answer almost all questions posed by instructor about the topic.	Student is able to accurately answer most questions posed by instructor about the topic.	Student is able to accurately answer a few questions posed by instructor about the topic.	Student is unable to accurately answer questions posed by instructor about the topic.	4

Relating benefits to customer needs	Student is completely prepared and has obviously rehearsed.	Student seems pretty prepared but might have needed a couple more rehearsals.	The student is somewhat prepared, but it is clear that rehearsal was lacking.	Student does not seem at all prepared to present.	3
Demonstrates knowledge of competition	Student is able to state three reasons why X company is better than the competition clearly and concisely.	Student is able to state clearly and concisely at least two reasons why X company is better than the competition.	Student is able to state two reasons why X company is better than competition but is somewhat unclear.	Student is able to state only one reason why X company is better than competition and is not clear in this description.	3
Case study	Excellent correlation of product benefits to customer problem	Good correlation of product benefits to customer problem	Some correlation of product benefits to customer problem; needs work	No correlation of product benefit to customer problem; confused	3

TOTAL SCORE_____17

Comments: John was able to demonstrate an understanding of the product features, functions, and benefits at a high level of detail. He was mostly clear as to how the benefits would help solve customer problems. He did correlate feature benefits as a solution to the case study presented and was prepared but seemed nervous and distracted. He described how the product fared against competitive offerings clearly. Recommendations: More practice of relating benefits to customer needs and continued learning as described in his individual training plan (ITP).

Surveys

Surveys should be distributed the week following the product training to all training attendees, including their managers, and submitted via regular mail or the Web (this is preferred method—Web surveys are much easier to collate, track, and compare results to earlier surveys). The surveys should be identical to the one given prior to the product training event. The participants should be given approximately two weeks to complete and submit the survey. As in the case of the pre-training survey distribution, two actions can occur to maximize survey return. The first is the announcement of a prize drawing from the pool of names submitting the survey. The prize should be sufficiently attractive to the target audience to warrant attention. Names are drawn at random from all who complete the survey. The number of prizes given out is determined by the number of training attendees. The second action to increase compliance is phone calls and e-mails to those that have not completed the survey. Training attendee managers can be used to further urge better return rate of surveys. The expected return rate using these tactics is at least 70 percent of the training attendees and 100 percent of the managers.

One option to ensure high returns is to hand out paper surveys at the end of training with the expectation the attendees will fill them out then and there and give them to logistics people stationed at the exits. The downfall of this approach is that the training managers or administrators will need to manually enter the data onto the Web site; this is neither cost-effective nor an efficient use of time.

Phase V—Continued

LEARNING AND PERIODIC ASSESSMENT

Continual learning is important in facilitating recall and retention of previously learned information. Continued learning and follow-up testing will help assure competency through repetition of vital material and better retention of information. "Performance assessment, support tools, and before-and-after learning events help salespeople and their managers to determine the impact of sales-related training and continue the development cycle long after an official training event ends" (Hall 2005). The short-term gains of face-to-face training must be turned into long-term gains through the use of continuing education. Adult students will return to their old habits and unlearn new techniques if allowed (Aronauer 2006). Quarterly training and periodic assessments are recommended to maintain competence and confidence in relating product value to customer needs. Continued learning after primary training sessions is effective through various blended learning methods.

Continued learning is vital for learning retention.

The first blended learning method is periodic classroom training. Some organizations have both central and field training managers and can offer regionally-based product training reinforcement or updates. Periodic classroom training should include blended learning techniques much like the main product training. Web- or computer-based pre-training assignments will ensure that the implementation of the small group, problem-based learning approach can be used. Classroom discussion can then be focused on applying and reinforcing learning.

Because quarterly face-to-face classroom training may not be possible due to time and geographic constraints, e-learning will provide the technology possible for continued reinforcement of the learned material from the initial, face-to-face training event. Technology-delivered courses allow for increased productivity (David 2006) because students can schedule their training sessions when they have the time. E-learning consists of webinars, webchats, and such applications on specified subjects. E-learning can also consist of virtual classrooms where videoconferencing is used to maintain the benefits of face-to-face training.

E-learning can be accomplished in many ways.

Webinars are an interactive way to provide distance training and workshops. Some webinars are asynchronous, that is, they do not take place in real time. Other webinars are "live;" that is, attendees log in at a specified time to receive lectures and participate in workshops through chat rooms or via simultaneous teleconferencing. Advantages and disadvantages can be found in both methods; thus, a live webinar can be recorded and archived for later viewing or reviewing. The information provided through the webinar consists of information provided from the main product training event. Brief product feature, function, and benefit reviews are followed by discussion. The segments, including the discussion section, are made available for viewing on the training department or LMS Web site. The segments are chunked into manageable sections in order to be downloaded to mobile learning devices such as iPODs. After each training segment, mini-testing can take place as a self-test to assess individual levels of learning.

A Word about Podcasting and Instant Messaging

Podcasting has become a major benefit to training because it provides a highly accessible, mobile learning technology that salespeople can use wherever they are, even if they are away from the ability to log onto a Web site (Hahn 2006). Podcasting is also beneficial in that the podcasts are typically recorded in shorter segments and thus provide smaller chunks of information for the salesperson to absorb, thereby increasing the retention of the learned information. Podcasts can either be directly downloaded from a training Web site or be downloaded automatically to an employee's portable media player device. The benefits to providing automatic downloads are that as new information or training content becomes available, the employee has immediate access to the information and does not have to take the time to search for updates.

Another way to provide rapid information to remote employees is instant messaging (IM). The advantage to this method is that it provides an easy way to communicate simple messages to anyone, anywhere. IM is especially useful for communicating "tips of the day" to people around the world, as the majority of countries, and all remote employees, have cell phone service. IM does have disadvantages. Security risks, such as leakage of competitive information and the potential of viral attacks, need to be carefully controlled and monitored.

Both podcasting and instant messaging offer quick and inexpensive ways to communicate tips and updates.

Implementing the Small Group, Problem-based Approach in Continued Learning

The small group, problem-based learning approach can be implemented within the e-learning environment. The CBT delivery method of learning has been described by Wheeler (2006) as a "version of PBL that can be offered to distance learners." The distance learning application of PBL is offered through the use of computer technology and the Web environment; students are able to easily access information and even collaborate through this delivery method. Web technology offers additional education by the opportunity for the learning teams to continue communication and to post new problems and potential solutions in a Web-forum type of environment. Real-life problem situations can be offered through "virtual portals" and presented to students anytime and anywhere. As in face-to-face PBL, students practice problem-solving skills at first on their own by investigating the scope and context of the problem. Online learning groups are formed and "encouraged to collaborate as a team with each member monitoring the progress of others while assessing their own" (Wheeler 2006). Online discussion groups are ideal environments to propagate individual learning through feedback from others.

Small group, problem-based learning can be readily implemented in the distance learning environment.

One way to use discussion groups to continue the learning from the main product training is to publish case studies of wins and losses. Online discussions of how the sales win was accomplished using the product feature/function/benefit training will help others try and even refine the same approach. These discussions can be live via a chat session and/or published on the training or LMS Web site for any employee to view worldwide. Chat sessions can be structured and/or scheduled or via blogging, something more companies are implementing on secure corporate Web servers. Online discussions do need to be monitored to assure appropriate content. A synopsis on the win discussions can easily be broadcast to a worldwide audience via instant messaging (IM).

A Web site should be available or created in order to easily track test scores and survey results along with profiles of all of the students. We have discussed the importance of having an LMS (Learning Management System). Assessment scores, survey results, and test scores can be stored and readily available for individual comparison. In addition, results can be viewed and compared between specified groups, such as sales regions or learning groups.

Individual Training Plans (ITP)

Because of the ability to compare pre- and post-training assessment scores and the documentation from the training facilitators on the assessment rubric, training plans can be developed for individual students. Training modules and courses of action can then be recommended for performance improvement. For example, a salesperson may have a good grasp of the product features and functions but may have a hard time addressing customer needs with the proposed solution using product benefits. The ITP would include a mentoring program, pairing the student with a more experienced salesperson to increase competence with customer solution selling.

Individual training plans should be created for all employees, archived on internal Web sites, and accessed through portals.

Periodic Assessments and Online Testing

To prove that continued learning and retention is happening, periodic testing and assessment is necessary. Online testing addresses product knowledge and application levels. Face-to-face assessment is good at testing actual ability to articulate product features, functions, and benefits to solve customer problems. Online testing is easier than face-to-face assessments and can be performed on a quarterly basis. Face-to-face performance assessment should be accomplished at least twice a year and can be performed on the regional or local level for remote employees. Online test and assessment scores will direct any changes to the individual training plan.

Another Word or Two on Assessments and Surveys

Evaluation of problem-based learning methods is more easily tracked through computer-based programs (Wheeler 2006). Tracking of student assessments, learning styles, and activities is easy to accomplish. Surveys of student satisfaction with the training are easily implemented. In addition, according to David (2006), "Web-based learning evaluation systems, often called analytics systems, can gauge the impact of an e-learning program by providing data and statistics that measure increases in sales, speed to competency, and customer satisfaction levels." Showing the return on problem-based learning and the resulting training investment is extremely hard to prove. Tracking test scores along with customer satisfaction levels can provide the necessary documentation to prove the effectiveness of sales training.

Chapter 5:

FORMATIVE AND SUMMATIVE EVALUATION

Evaluation of the program curriculum and instruction is vital to the success of the training outcomes. Both formative and summative evaluations are necessary to ensure both that the training meets the learning needs of the students and that all stakeholders share the desired outcome. Evaluation thus is vital to validate the curriculum. Both types of evaluation need to occur within any training program.

Formative Evaluation

Formative evaluation is the examination of curriculum development from inception through implementation and includes the consideration of stakeholders' concerns and needs. Stakeholders need to be involved in the strategic planning of any training program if improvements are to be realized (Hayes 2003). At the start of product training planning (up to six months before the actual training event, depending on the scope of training), goals are set for the training, and instructional strategy is then discussed. For example, I changed my training strategy a few years ago from large audience format to a small group, problem-based learning approach after stakeholders, including the vice president of sales, complained about "death by PowerPoint." The instruction may not be aligned with the curriculum goals if stakeholders' input is not sought. Formative evaluation ensures that the training goals and objectives are matched to the business initiatives.

Actively listening to stakeholder input is critical to the success of any training program.

Formative evaluation consists of the process of assessing instructional material in the design process. Evaluation during the formation of the instructional design is necessary because the designer may inadvertently include flaws or unfinished areas within the design itself that could be averted with formative evaluation. This process will assist the trainer in successfully implementing any program, especially if that program is a new concept for the training department, has never been implemented in the past, and will be highly visible to senior management. Formative evaluation will help fine-tune the program through the completion of its four stages.

Program curriculum is greatly enhanced through thoughtful formative evaluation.

The first stage of a formative evaluation is reviewing the design itself to ensure that the program goals, objectives, and learner and environmental context are all in line with the instructional design. The needs assessment is one area that will fulfill the first stage goals. The participants in this stage include the training director and any stakeholder directly involved with the training outcome. The second stage includes the review of the instructional design by experts in the field. Participants in this stage include the training personnel, who are subject matter experts, and an instructional designer within or outside of the company. In addition, any other trainer connected to the learners will be included to make sure the level of instruction is adequate. For example, if the learners are sales representatives, then field sales trainers will be included in the planning.

The third stage of formative evaluation is validation by the learners (Rothwell, et al. 2002, p. 185) and will include rehearsing the program with a few representative members of the target audience. The purpose of this evaluation is to receive feedback from the participants on the clarity of instruction and understanding of content. For example, the content may assume knowledge or vocabulary that the training participants do not have. Because of the feedback, the invalid assumption would be brought to light and the instructional content revised. The fourth and last stage involves ongoing evaluation that includes an assessment of a small group of targeted employees to check if the revisions made during the prior stages meet the target audience needs. The benefit of this evaluation is that it examines how well the instruction works with learners of wide experience and how effective the program will be without the designer's direct presence.

The final formative evaluation report takes place at least one month before implementation of the training program. The results will be presented to the training personnel and all stakeholders to ensure adequate communication of the status of the design of the learning program. The meeting on formative results will bring everyone to the same level of understanding on the project goals and intended outcomes. At this point, any changes to the curriculum should be minor.

Formative evaluation is essential in garnering stakeholders' support of program implementation.

Summative Evaluation

Summative evaluation is the examination of overall program value and includes assessments needed to evaluate the effectiveness of the instruction. Summative evaluation includes stakeholder surveys, as well as any written test scores and performance-based assessment of the students. Resources to develop and implement instructional strategies that align with standards-based curriculum and reflect formative and summative evaluation are needed to properly monitor the initial phases of a curriculum/instruction alignment. Course correction is easier to implement if resources are readily available. Ewing (2003) has advocated dedicated resources to hold curriculum audits, which is a tool to manage the alignment of curriculum and instruction. The tool is expensive and demands dedicated resources. Since the alignment may take significant time to come to fruition, a pilot program would assess the effectiveness of the tool being undertaken as a test. The result is meant as "data-driven decision making for more effective instruction" (Ewing 2003).

Summative evaluation is a necessary and important component of this learning program because the stakeholders will closely examine the analysis of how effectively the program meets the objectives. Based on the positive outcome of the summative evaluation, the training program may be offered to other departments within the organization.

Summative evaluation assesses the qualitative and quantitative effectiveness of instruction.

Summative evaluation will benefit the program in many ways. The first way is that in analyzing the data you can make necessary adjustments to the program to increase its effectiveness. By demonstrating the benefits the program has to offer, other departments within the corporation will be interested in offering this program to their employees. In addition, the other divisions may implement this program to increase their knowledge level of the product. For example, product training programs targeted at salespeople may be of benefit for other departments, such as human resources and engineering.

The type of summative evaluation that will be used should include both objectivism and subjectivism. Both methods of evaluation can offer benefits in reviewing the effectiveness of the course. Using objective (SCAM) criteria, the test results should be analyzed to determine if the course objectives were met from a data-driven point of view. For example, approximately one month after the completion of the course, the participants may be required to take an online test similar to a test given at the conclusion of the course. A brief survey will be included at the same time to receive feedback on the course satisfaction from the viewpoint of the participant. This feedback will be used to determine future course enhancements. The training department and pertinent stakeholders should analyze both types of evaluations.

The summative evaluation should take place approximately one month following the conclusion of the learning program, when the program students will have completed the post-program online tests and surveys. The steps in the summative evaluation process should be followed carefully to ensure complete coverage. The first step is to determine the goals of the evaluation (Rothwell, et al. 2002). The reason for this stage is to determine the questions that need to be addressed as part of the evaluation. The topic for questions includes goal achievement, return on investment, and learner satisfaction. The second step is to identify how success of the program will be indicated as compared to the program objectives. Components include learning retention, transfer of information, benefit to the company, and any other benefit that could be identified as an outcome of achieving the program's goals.

The third step is to decide on the orientation, which is determined by discussing the attributes of using both quantitative and/or qualitative data as evidence of program success (Rothwell, et al. 2002). Both qualitative and quantitative data should be used in the training program as documented in the test and survey results. The next step is in determining the actual design that the evaluation should include. The data that is collected as part of the testing and survey is based on the needs assessment. Validity is then discussed and documented as part of the evaluation. Identifying alternative designs is also used in this process.

Summative evaluation consists of an analysis of survey results and assessment scores.

The measures of evaluation and outcomes are the next steps and will be described within this summative evaluation. The measure will include test result data as an objective measure and survey results as subjective measure. The collection, analysis, and reporting of the data will prove the measure of evaluation and outcomes. This is an important step in determining the quality and transfer of learned material. Results indicated in this step indicate whether the objectives of the training were met and to what degree.

Chapter 6:

DOCUMENTING OUTCOMES

Documenting outcomes is perhaps the least understood and least utilized part of corporate product training programs. Most product training is performed as a one-time event with minimal documentation of the outcome of the training. Many product training programs are reactive to a short-term, immediate need. Some managers confuse return on investment (ROI) with the expected training outcome. While not mutually exclusive, most training programs document outcomes in the form of survey, testing, and/or assessment results. In order to effectively communicate the expected and realized outcomes of any educational program, one must first know what outcome is expected from and agreed to by the stakeholders of the training.

Why Document Outcomes?

The first reason to document outcomes is to demonstrate an increase in student satisfaction, confidence, and self-efficacy after attending product training. Most outcome documentation that is historically performed is usually in the form of a survey. Determining the reaction of the student to a training program can provide valuable information to enhance future programs. If students have positive reactions to a training event, then it is more likely that they will be more open to learning concepts, are more alert, and will have greater personal accountability. Though learning is not assured, it is more readily attained if students are comfortable and satisfied with their learning experience.

Surveys provide an indicator of student reaction and satisfaction with training program implementation.

The second (and very important) reason to document outcomes is to prove that learning is occurring. Survey results are a valuable and necessary first step in the learning process, but they are limited in that they indicate only the reaction of attendees and overall satisfaction with the training program. Surveys reflect the Kirkpatrick Level 1 of learning and should be the first, but not the only, indicator of successful training (see appendix B for an overview of the Kirkpatrick levels of learning). A higher level of learning needs to be attained to ensure that the knowledge is acquired for the student to competently understand and articulate product features, functions, and benefits.

Training success is based not only on student satisfaction but on a higher level of student learning. If a student is happy with the training program but hasn't learned anything, what's the purpose of training? Assuring and documenting that learning has occurred is a necessary step in attaining and maintaining product training excellence. Proving that learning has occurred can be documented using standard written testing and performance assessments. Some training departments use written tests only to document level of knowledge. While this is fine to prove that the student understands the product basics, best practices indicate that adding performance assessment using oral presentations is the best way to assure a higher and more effective level of learning—and thus a better ability to communicate product value to potential customers.

A combination of testing and performance assessments is the best way to prove a higher level of learning.

Another reason that the documentation of training outcomes is essential is to prove the skills that the student learned during the training session and then use that information to create an individual training plan. Using the results from the assessments, the student's manager can provide individual plans for that student, including additional areas of study (e.g., presentation skills workshops) and other areas for improvement. This is especially important for the newer employee or for employees who need to improve their performance.

The fourth reason to document outcomes is to show that management is satisfied with the results of product training. To be honest, upper management may not be interested in the specifics of product training and how much employees are learning. Some managers want to see results but not necessarily how the results were achieved. Results may be in the form of increased sales. We know that many factors impact selling; effective product training is but one. If management demands hard data, steps need to be taken to perform extensive analysis using quantitative data tools, control groups, etc., for the most defensible results. Demonstrating this kind of ROI is not feasible in most organizations because of the difficulty and expense.

However, general observations and descriptions can be provided to management and, if matched with online assessment and sales tracking, demonstrate the connection between learning and increased sales or efficiencies. Learning initiatives should be shown to match to business goals (Naughton 2008). Naughton also suggests that success stories can demonstrate the impact of learning. Thus, the continued learning programs that were described in chapter 5, using learning groups to discuss product wins and losses, can be a valuable source of data when presenting learning benefits to management. Frequent communication on outcomes of product training and relating those outcomes to business goals is imperative to demonstrate the impact of learning.

Impact of learning programs in the sales environment can be demonstrated in part through win/loss reporting.

Data-driven Outcome Analysis Using Direct ROI

Most of the documented learning outcomes discussed thus far involve qualitative analysis and descriptions. Some organizations may want the training department to prove a business impact of learning for executive management. As we all know, many factors can impact business results aside from product training programs. However, proving a return on the investment in the training program may be directed to the training leader; thus a need may exist for directly tying learning solutions to business objectives and initiatives. Proving that the learning outcome directly impacts business results is possible but involves a substantial investment in complex statistical analysis software and the probable need for control groups. Some professional learning organizations, such as Chief Learning Officer (CLO) and Bellevue University, deal directly with measuring ROI, something outside the scope of this book.

Debra J. Smith

Data-driven Decision Making

Data-driven decision making has become a buzzword in school systems and is becoming a key component of some learning organizations. But data-driven decision making is becoming an important part of quality assurance in many learning organizations. Going far beyond the accountability demanded by an organization's learning standards (if they exist), the process of evaluating objective data ensures higher quality learning for employees. Data-driven decision making is the process of collecting objective data and analyzing it in order to positively impact the performance of learning organizations and the learning of its employees. Several benefits of data-driven decision making can be identified, as well as pitfalls that can undermine its value.

Data-driven decision making can add value beyond simple accountability. It is imperative that accountability be measured to the quality of learning beyond simple testing in order to positively impact the future of learning organizations. One way to do this is through data analysis, an objective way to assess an organization's learning performance.

Several steps are needed to implement a data-driven process and make it effective in the learning organization. The process starts through the incorporation of technology and data analysis resource allocation. Next, data analysis systems, as well as resources to help training departments learn to interpret the data, are needed to start the active implementation of this process. Thirdly, the training department needs to determine what data is to be acquired and analyzed. For example, student (employee) assessments can be analyzed from test and performance data; thus administrative efficiencies, such as targeting only those individuals that need additional training, can be determined from operational data. However, to successfully implement this plan, learning organizations need to integrate data from both administrative and curricular entities.

Data-driven decision making can go beyond accountability information and can include important information such as trends in demographics, administrative budget analysis, and trainer/instructor development needs. Thus data-driven decision making can transform student learning, trainer satisfaction, and training department efficiency. For example, if the data determined a trend that showed an increase in the number of international (and non-English-speaking) students enrolling per year, as seen in most global organizations, the training department could forecast the need for additional resources, such as translation services, well in advance of the actual need.

Data-driven decision making could also impact the big-picture strategy created by the learning organization's senior management, such as the chief learning officer (CLO). Instead of evaluating the day-to-day operations of the training department, senior management could ubiquitously analyze multiple data points and set the organization's overall learning strategy and resource forecasting to meet employee and training department needs. This is already incorporated in many areas of the business world. The efficiencies that have been demonstrated in businesses, such as increased profits and cost savings, are known to have come from companies tirelessly performing data-driven decision making through careful data analysis.

Data-driven decision making does have its limitations. As long as the data can be used to improve the learning process, its value is limitless. However, when the data is misused or interpreted incorrectly, it can be detrimental to the learning organization. For example, the data needs to serve the purpose of the question asked. If there is a misunderstanding of what the data's specific purpose is, then the users will perceive this process as worthless. Some learning organizations and trainers have been resistant to data-driven decision making. Many trainers see this process as a way to criticize their teaching abilities and perceive it as a way to complicate, not simplify, their lives. The data obtained will have to become a daily part of their lives, as well as and easy to use and interpret, for trainers to embrace this process.

In the sales environment, data-driven decision making in product training is in its infancy in most organizations. Data should be obtained regarding the new sales representative's demographics and sales and product knowledge. Data is obtained through market analysis to determine the highest impact areas of sales focus. For example, it may be determined to focus on hospitals instead of physician private practices in some areas of the world. Since sales strategy is different in these markets, the data would point toward training to the hospital market customer needs.

Most sales organizations seldom use data-driven decision making in training programs.

Data-driven decision making is a worthwhile process because it adds objectivity to the process of evaluating quality in learning organizations. Accountability through testing itself is not enough; hard data that demonstrates areas for improvement is needed to prove the need for change to learning organizations, trainers, and senior management.

The fourth and final reason to document the outcomes from product training is to prove that the shift to small group problem-based learning really works. Implementing the small group, problem-based learning technique in product training programs requires a major paradigm shift in thinking. It may also require some investment in resources for effective implementation. Demonstrating the differences in survey results, testing, and performance-based assessments may be necessary to prove value to senior management.

How Do We Measure Outcomes?

Data collection instruments include surveys, testing, and assessment studies and take place some time prior to implementing the product training event. A second survey and assessment takes place immediately following the product training. The survey is used to describe the beliefs and attitudes of the students and managers regarding the quality of product training and the impact of that training on their ability to competently and confidently communicate product features and benefits to customers. Students have the opportunity to add their own comments within the survey. For example, the pre-training survey results may document that a problem exists through the lack of confidence felt by employees in the training techniques targeted at increasing their competence in presenting product features and benefits to customers. The training or LMS Web site should be used as the primary delivery method for the survey and should include a pilot test as an indicator of appropriateness.

Assessment studies of the students' ability to demonstrate competence in presenting product value provide data to demonstrate a baseline level of knowledge prior to new product or upgrade training implementation. The evaluator for the assessment studies should provide additional comments as to employee confidence and competence during the assessments.

The survey data that is collected is the direct responses to the survey questions provided by the participating students and their managers (see appendix D: Helpful Templates). Additional descriptive data is collected from the surveys, and a section for additional comments is provided. Using narrative analysis of the observed differences is essential in order to fully understand all nuances of the information obtained from the survey. These narrative discussions included the observed differences in survey answers for all ten questions. For example, in the pre-training survey, most of the students and their managers may like the past training formats. Learners may not even believe that the training would positively impact their sales numbers. The importance of this cannot be overstated; the responsibility of the training team is to effectively train so that employees such as salespeople can realize increased sales successes. The confidence of the learner in presenting product features and benefits increases self-efficacy, which is discussed in chapter 3 and in appendix C.

The assessment results are tabulated and analyzed through comparative tables and narrative examination. Percent increase or decrease between pre- and post-training assessment results are analyzed and discussed. The assessment results primarily look at the measures of central tendency, since the total scores of the data sets are averaged for the study participants. A histogram or bar graph can be used to provide a graphical summary of the distribution of the values in a data set along its range (table 5).

Table 5. Histogram of frequency of assessment score groups.

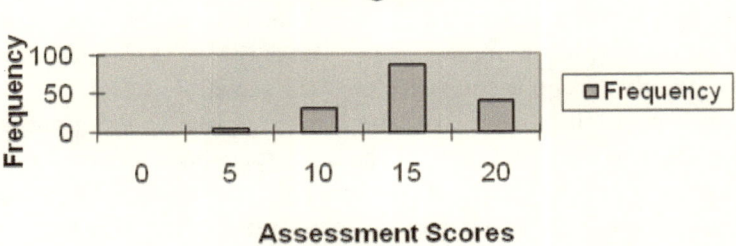

The histogram describes the frequency of occurrence in each class and is a visual representation of the frequency distribution of the assessment scores. Discussion of the reasons for any assessment result changes should be reviewed and discussed in depth. Additional comments from the evaluator are used to provide richer depth of discussion.

Validity of the qualitative data is seen as the extent to which the outcomes observed from the research are reasonable and appropriate. Reducing as much as possible the sources of potential measurement error maximizes reliability. This includes ensuring the scoring procedures are identical for pre-and post-implementation assessments, minimizing ambiguity in any wording in the survey, and assessment and taking inter-observer variability into account and considering the use of one scorer in assessment studies.

As is the problem with all qualitative studies, a potential bias may exist due to the influence of the assessor or survey analyst. As well, potential bias could be present in the survey design and interpretation of assessment results. To minimize the potential bias, two trainers should finalize the survey design and be present at all assessments. All training managers should provide independent analysis of the qualitative data.

The results of the data are evaluated using primarily qualitative methods using descriptive statistics. Quantitative data is used in order to provide comparisons between the pre-and post-training survey results and assessment scores. A discussion of analyzed data should be provided for each of the observed outcomes.

Graphs and charts are used to visually display training outcomes.

The data from the assessments can be disaggregated and the individual student's test information reviewed. Graphs can be used to better display the data to visually compare pre- and post-implementation data for the students. To examine the results more closely, the data may also be compiled into four groups. The first group is composed of students with less than two years of experience who fail baseline assessment testing. The second group should be comprised of the remainder of the less experienced students who pass assessment testing. The third group is comprised of students with greater than two years of experience who fail baseline assessment testing. The fourth group is the remaining experienced students who pass baseline assessment testing. A narrative discussion accompanies all assessment comparisons and includes any individual or group comments from the training managers.

Results from students and their managers should be kept separate. Comparisons between the two can prove to provide valuable information.

What Outcomes Do We Want?

The following are examples of a hypothetical outcome for a product training program:
1. All (100 percent) of managers and the majority of students are satisfied with the level of skill they have in discussing product features, functions, and benefits.
2. All (100 percent) of managers and the majority of students are satisfied with the quality and format of product training provided.

3. At least 65 percent of students with less than two years'
    experience are able to adequately address customer needs
    as demonstrated by passing performance assessment testing
    immediately after product training classes.
4. At least 80 percent of students with more than two years'
    experience are able to adequately address customer needs
    as demonstrated by passing performance assessment testing
    immediately after product training classes.

The first anticipated result is that 100 percent of managers and the majority of students should be satisfied with the level of skill they have in discussing product features, functions, and benefits. The first goal is directly measured by positive responses to the questions on the distributed survey. As a reminder, the survey ideally should be distributed via the Web and the link e-mailed to all students and their managers attending the training session. The body of the survey includes statements relating to the effectiveness of the training session that the salesperson can agree or disagree with. For example, one statement may be, "After training, the students will be able to confidently and competently explain the new features and present the product effortlessly to customers." The students rate their answers as "strongly agree," "agree," "neutral," "disagree," or "strongly disagree." The majority (over 75 percent) of the students should respond positively to the new training format and quality to mark training success. Of the people responding neutrally to the survey, years of experience should be examined; those with less than two years' experience may incorporate the majority of these responders. Another expected result is that all of the students' managers should respond positively to this question on the survey.

The second anticipated result is that 100 percent of managers and the majority of students should be satisfied with the format of sales training provided. This outcome is achieved as measured by positive responses to the questions on the distributed survey. For example, one statement may be, "The small size of the learning groups was an advantage." The students rate their answers as "strongly agree," "agree," "neutral," "disagree," or "strongly disagree." The majority (over 75 percent) of the students should respond positively to the new training format and quality to mark training success. Any additional comments from the students, their managers, and training personnel should be included within the discussion as needed.

The third anticipated result is that at least 65 percent of people with less than two years' experience should be able to adequately address customer needs.

The outcome is successful by the students demonstrating passing scores on training assessments given immediately following product training classes. The pre-and post-assessment scores should be compared to see if the product training had a positive impact on test scores. The students in this group should have more passing scores as compared to the passing scores prior to the new product training and are expected to indicate increased effectiveness of product training.

The last anticipated result is that 80 percent of students with more than two years' experience should be able to adequately address customer needs by using product features/functions/benefits. The last outcome is reached and documented by passing scores on training assessments given immediately following product training classes.

Showing the final outcomes to stakeholders can be easily demonstrated via a table (see table 6). Remember that any written tests reflect Kirkpatrick Level 2 of learning. Performance assessments (Kirkpatrick Level 3) enhance learning and consist of a face-to-face practical examination that measures student knowledge in effectively relating product features, functions, and benefits to customer situations. Passing the assessment is indicated by a total score of 15 or higher. The baseline test assessments are performed before product training on the student population and demonstrate the data for students with less than two years' experience that failed the assessment (table 6).

Table 6. A template for individual score total by group types of learners

Learning Groups	Years of experience	Individual score totals
Group A N=w	< two years	<15
Group B N=x	< two years	>15
Group C N=y	> two years	<15
Group D N=z	> two years	>15

The results should indicate that more of the experienced students pass the after-training performance assessments, as compared to the percentage of passing assessment scores prior to the implementation of the new product training. In other words, each training event or assessment should build upon the last. Students are expected to increase their abilities as time progresses.

Results should confirm that the implementation of the phased approach incorporating small group, problem-based learning techniques into the product training classes increase the competence and confidence of sales team members in communicating product value to customers in a way in which the customers can relate.

Conclusion

Improving the quality of the training programs is provided from analyzing the documented learning outcomes. Much information can be gleaned from surveys; more can be obtained through the tracking of test and assessment scores. Tracking survey results, test scores, and assessment results significantly improves the ability of the training department to refine and redirect training efforts. Future product training can be greatly enhanced by thorough review of such information.

Chapter 7:

LOGISTICAL CONSIDERATIONS

Logistics are an important factor to be taken into consideration in implementing any product training program and especially with the five phase approach using small group, problem-based learning. The instructional design, though sharing the same learning objectives, will be different than that used with a conventional training approach. Physical space may need to be modified, as well as classroom setup.

Classroom Setup

Conventional training classrooms within organizational departments will need to be converted to classrooms that can support small learning groups. This should be easy if the existing learning space consists of regular rooms; if the classroom is a lecture theater then alternative solutions will need to be found. The size of the class depends on the size of the classroom space and the number of trainers available. Usually classes within organizations are of limited size. For example, new-hire product training classes generally are limited to approximately twenty students for a room size of 40 by 40 feet. Each learning group has four to five team members. The middle space of the learning group is reserved for the product to be trained on for demonstration and practice purposes. The area needed for the team of four is approximately 8 by 8 feet. Figure 1 illustrates a typical setup of a 40-feet by 40-feet classroom using learning groups. The break area should be located outside of the classroom.

Figure 1. General classroom setup using small learning group approach

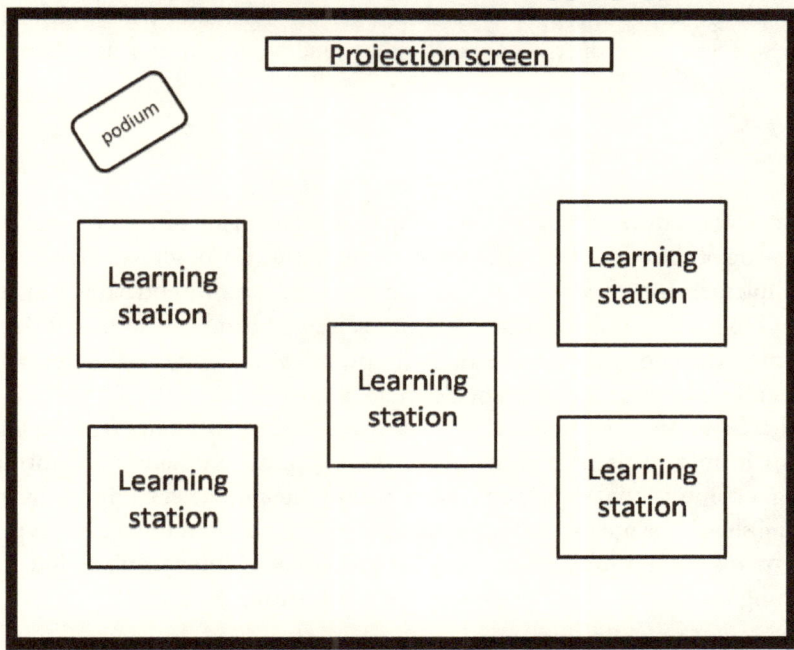

Figure 2. Detailed view of classroom setup

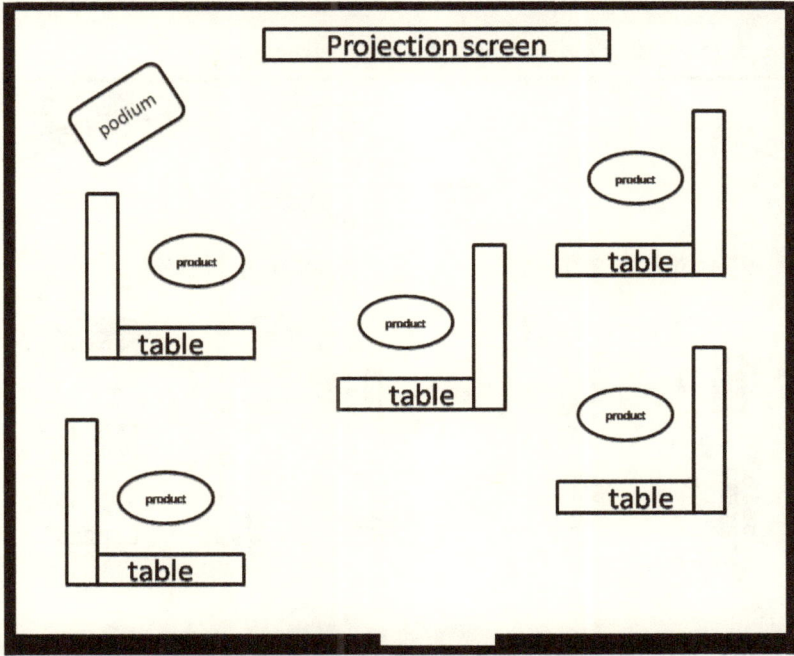

One instructor and an additional two facilitators are ideal for a twenty-person class. The general philosophy of facilitation is one facilitator per two learning groups. Depending on the course content, one facilitator can handle up to three groups.

New Product Training

Most new product or upgrade trainings for sales organizations consist of a gathering of the entire field sales force, either nationally or globally. The result of implementing this new training format and accommodating learning groups for such training is that the venue selected must be of sufficient size to accommodate not only the learning groups, but also a stage and presentation area and audiovisual center. For example, a sales force of 100 to 120 would need a ballroom approximately 100 feet by 70 feet to handle the learning group format. This is slightly larger than typical large audience formats using a conventional classroom setup. Ceiling height is very important; the ceiling should be no lower than 14 by 16 feet. Figure 3 demonstrates a typical ballroom setup for product training for a group of 112 people using fourteen learning stations (maximum of 8 people per learning group).

Coffee breaks should take place outside the classroom; hotels usually provide foyer areas outside of ballrooms for this purpose.

Figure 3. Example of a room layout for new product training

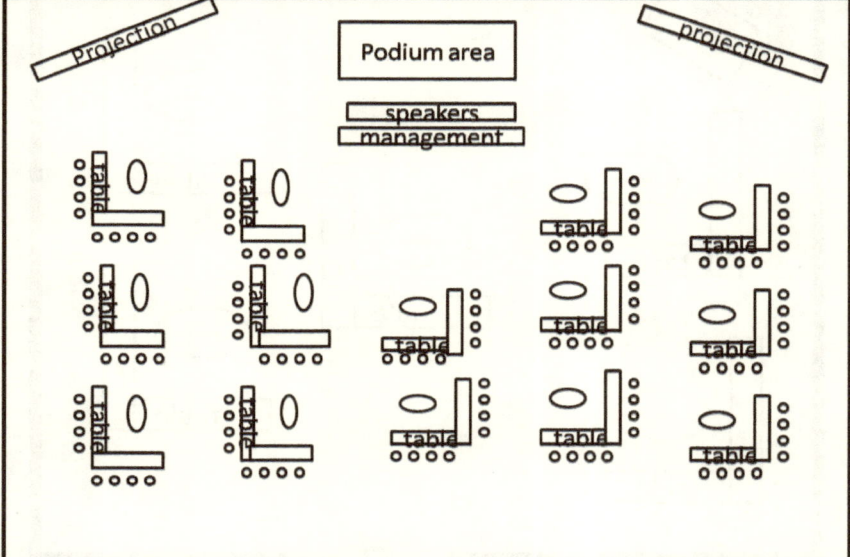

Instructional Materials

Perhaps the most significant logistical change in implementing the five phases approach to training and specifically to the small group, problem-based learning technique is in the design and development of instructional materials. Instructional materials for pre-training assignments need to focus on knowledge transfer and use multimedia to increase learner interest. As in any other instructional design, learner characteristics and learning styles should be included when designing pre-training instructional materials.

Since online pre-training assignments for a product training event have prepared the students with a basic product overview (technology and features), the classroom time can focus on how best to present the technology and features in a way customers can relate to and ultimately buy. Instructional materials for the classroom using small group, problem-based learning are significantly different than what is currently used in many product training classes. Classroom time should be approximately 25 percent lecture and 75 percent workshops and/or discussion groups. Training material needs to be changed accordingly. The lecture portion, easily accomplished through PowerPoint presentation, is purposefully simple and straightforward, with the objective of setting up the discussion group topics. Discussion group topics range from a product demonstration to set up the day(s) of training to discussing the benefits each feature will bring to a customer. The trainers should work closely with management to obtain sufficient numbers of problem-based customer scenarios for new product and new-hire training.

Workbook size needs to be kept to a minimum; detailed enough to help the facilitator guide but vague enough not to provide easy answers for the students. The workbook can be simply composed of "think sheets"—questions to keep discussions on the right track.

Learning group members should be worked out before the product training commences. Employees with more than two years' experience should be partnered with newer employees. In cases of sales training, keeping regions together can add to the value of the discussion groups because customers' preferences will help tame any logistical concerns. It can take up to six months to find a training venue (usually in a hotel) for a large product training rollout. Involving stakeholders from the inception of meetings will help smooth out logistical issues that are bound to arise. Creation of a detailed product training plan with a timeline of events included is helpful to ensure nothing falls between the cracks.

It is important to strategically think of the individuals who should be placed together in learning groups.

Distance Learning

Invest in a Learning Management System (LMS) system if you haven't already. An LMS is essential for continued learning and tracking of student progress. Investment in this type of technology is essential for any training program to become successful. Pre-training assignments and testing can be delivered via the Web or by DVD. Any presentations can be archived on a Web site for later review by students. Test and assessment scores can be tracked and individual student plans can be maintained. The process to select an LMS can be lengthy, so until an LMS is available you can use a corporate training Web site to achieve your short-term goals.

Chapter 8:

CHALLENGES AND SOLUTIONS

Several challenges can be identified that face the implementation of the five phase approach to product training. The first is the challenge of change itself. The second is the design, development, and implementation of the curriculum. The third pertains to logistical issues that may be encountered. This chapter identifies the components of the challenges and reveals simple solutions that dissolve implementation issues.

Becoming an Agent of Change

Everyone knows that change can be intimidating. Changing the mindset of both learner and management can be daunting. Change can be especially hard for people that have been doing things the same way throughout their lives, thus most people are adverse to change. Reasons for this vary, but in general, learning new ideas, especially those that are complex, can be difficult, and most people are afraid of failure. The very threat of failure is enough for some people to stubbornly and passionately resist change. However, since you are reading this book you must have either surveyed or heard from learners in your organization that they are not happy with the current state of training (e.g., "death by PowerPoint"), or you know yourself that product training can be better than it has been. You know that some kind of change is needed in the way employees are trained on new products or upgrades—otherwise why read further? Thus you have to be an agent for change. Once people see, understand, and embrace the need for change, they are more likely to accept it. It is your responsibility to lead them through. Let's now discuss some of the challenges you may face in implementing this paradigm shift in learning.

Change is stressful for most people.

Stakeholders are people too and may be adverse to change.
Any person supporting the product training initiatives and ensuring compliance in their employees for learning are referred to as "stakeholders." Some stakeholders are interested in increasing the effectiveness of their employees and determining if the program was worth the time and money spent. Other stakeholders, such as those in the training department, are interested in determining the effectiveness of the program to determine areas for design improvement. Yet other stakeholders will want to be assured that the investment made in designing and implementing the programs has good return. Thus, stakeholders need to be involved from the beginning of the product training strategy and kept informed throughout.

Stakeholders can make or break a great training program!

If management, particularly sales management, does not have a close partnership or a level of trust with the training department, they will probably be reluctant to try new training strategies. In addition, managers will desire involvement in their employees' learning and development (and rightly so). If they do not feel that they have input into some areas of the product training strategy, they will probably not have open minds when presented with the final plan. Great communication and networking with key stakeholders is vital to ensure the smooth implementation of any great training program. Stakeholders need to be informed through each phase of product training (see chapter 5).

Communication, communication, communication! The more that stakeholders are involved in training strategy discussions, the more that they will be likely to see the advantages of change.

Most employees are used to product training as a one-time occurrence.
The challenge with training on complex products, such as medical device systems, is that they contain advanced core technologies; many features and benefits can be determined based on each core technology. Because human beings tend to retain no more than half of what they experience during one product overview presentation, additional methods of knowledge transfer or learning strategies are demanded. Using pre-training assignments as a basis

for knowledge retention, classroom-based training for knowledge application, and distance learning for follow-up is a logical approach and can ensure up to 90 percent learning retention.

Continued learning (and repetition!) dramatically increases retention and easier recall of learned information.

Adults are used to the passive learning style of large audiences.
Most adult learners in corporations are taught new ideas via the lecture theater. These adult learners were most likely taught in the same way throughout their primary school and college years. Thus most are comfortable (though bored and impatient), sitting through endless product training lectures using conventional and passive learning techniques. The transition from a large audience to small, problem-based learning group is a paradigm shift that may create a feeling of insecurity with students (Miflin 2004), particularly at the beginning of the implementation. Collaboration with others in addition to self-study will support students as they transition to the new format of learning. Miflin (2004) states "the support of a tutor and group of peers helps students to develop the security and authority they need to be responsible for their own learning." Guidance for students in new learning situations is more readily facilitated in small groups, where the teacher-to-student ratio is lower (Miflin 2004).

Learning group members need to support each other through the classroom experience.

As Raucent (2001) remarks, "There is a marked difference between what a teacher speaks about during a lecture and what students really absorb." Raucent goes on to state, "Students retain 10 percent of what they read, 26 percent of what they hear, 30 percent of what they see, 50 percent of what they see and hear, 70 percent of what they say, and 90 percent of what they say as they do something."

When evaluating the impact of product training using active learning techniques, the learning impact may not be distinguished from the newness of the small group, problem-based learning format. That is, the use of small learning groups is such a departure from the classic large audience format that the students may react to that and not the small group, problem-based learning approach. However, the use of assessment results when discussing outcomes provides a concrete example of the value of both problem-based learning and the use of small learning groups in the learning process.

Students will have increased attention and interest due in part to the newness and format of the learning group technique.

Facilitation of group learning is highly dependent on the facilitator.
Facilitation of the small group, problem-based learning approach does have its challenges. One of the main tasks of a tutor is to successfully facilitate group discussion and learning (Azer 2005). The role of a facilitator is to encourage group discussion by identifying open-ended questions. The facilitator is not present to provide answers or lecture on pertinent topics. Rather, the facilitator creates a comfortable and easy learning environment and acts as a guide to help the learning group achieve their goals. The facilitator also is charged with keeping the learning group focused on the task or problem to be solved.

As Azer (2005) states, "Facilitation is not about detailed content or what the group works on, it is more about how the group approaches big concepts, how it identifies open-ended questions that encourage group discussion, and how the group members identify their learning needs." Facilitation of the small-sized, problem-based learning group means to keep the group focused on the task at hand and acts more as a guide to enable critical thinking about the problem and potential solutions. Facilitators have to take care not to dominate group discussion and provide ready answers when the group appears to be stuck. Asking open-ended questions may help to expand discussion and foster group-centered learning.

The role of the learning group facilitator is to maintain focus and encourage dialogue.

Employees are not used to performance-based assessments after product training.
Employees are used to filling out surveys after product training and, at the most, a brief written test. They are not used to assessments, especially those that are performance-based. The first performance assessment I initiated after I applied small group, problem-based learning to sales training was met with shocked looks on the faces of the salespeople. The salespeople were uncomfortable with having such assessments imposed upon them, even after they were informed *weeks* before the product training commenced. Some salespeople are uncomfortable being assessed in front of their peers; however,

the vast majority of these people were glad that they had such an assessment because they felt much more comfortable when presenting in front of their customers.

The use of performance-based assessments within learning groups provides a valuable way not only to learn from others but also to practice before presenting in front of an actual customer.

Curricular Challenges

Small group, problem-based learning is not without its critics, though most of these critics seem to accept the philosophical value of the problem-based learning concept. The disagreements are with the practices within the technique, such as the curricular design and implementation (Fenwick 2002). Several factors impact the analysis, design, development, implementation, and evaluation of the product training curriculum.

The alignment between curriculum and instruction is vital to ensure that goals and objectives of the training are communicated to students in a way that is meaningful and can be retained. The process of alignment needs to be undertaken carefully and thoughtfully. All stakeholders need to understand this process and communicate best practices to ensure a successful outcome. To understand the relationship between curriculum and instruction, one must first understand what each means.

The alignment of curriculum and instruction is vital to effective learning outcomes. Instruction is the process of *how* the curriculum content is taught. Curriculum is *what* is taught.

Instruction can be performed in many ways. Large group instruction is more passive and consists of lecture and class discussion. Small group instruction is naturally more active in that more discussion and critical thinking exercises can be implemented. One-on-one instruction, or tutorials, is focused on individual student needs and is usually performed outside of regular classroom sessions.

Instructional strategy can be individualistic in the approach a teacher takes to teaching the curriculum. For example, in medical schools, strategy leans toward problem-based exercises; in most corporations the strategy leans toward intense didactic sessions. In either institution, the instruction should be based on curriculum content. For example, if the section of training is on product technology, only then can the curricular content focus more on multimedia instruction and less on problem-based learning. If the training component is on features and benefits, then the instruction needs to focus on discussion groups and less on didactic presentation.

Curriculum is what is taught in the classroom. Expectations for each student or group of students are included within training goals and guidelines and curriculum material is written directly from those expectations. Too often training is a reactive action to external forces.

The alignment between curriculum and instruction can be accomplished through several stages. The first stage is to understand the requirements in the form of training initiatives. Training initiatives are based on marketing initiatives and business goals. These initiatives are then used as points of reference when designing curriculum and developing instructional strategies.

The second stage is to match the curricular goals with the instructional strategy. According to Hayes (2003), "Without common and agreed goals, instructors are forced to work in isolation, acting upon what they consider to be important learning goals." The objectives based on the learning goals drive the training materials, instructional content and procedures, and the assessments that are created (Hayes 2003). To facilitate instructional development, some organizations have a centralized curricular framework in place that could be an important resource for those planning instruction (Browder, Spooner, Wakeman, Trela, and Baker 2006). However, it is the instructors (trainers) who develop and implement the instruction in the classroom. Thus, instructors need skills that allow them to be flexible to address the broad range of academic capabilities that adult student groups demonstrate.

The third stage is to evaluate if curriculum and instruction are to be aligned. Both formative and summative evaluations need to take place to ensure that the alignment is meeting the needs for both student and business objectives.

Some factors can influence an existing curriculum and subtly impact and underlie what students learn and experience above the goals and objectives that exist to serve the approved curriculum.

This is what is called a "hidden curriculum." According to Dekle (2004), "The hidden curriculum refers to the knowledge, beliefs, attitudes, behaviors, and rules that students internalize about a university, both intended and unintended." According to Bennett et al. (2004), "[Hidden curriculum] is a set of [sometimes unwritten] rules, routines, and regulations that exert a strong influence on learning and its application in practice."

Learning groups can influence a hidden curriculum in a number of ways. In some instances, a clear leader can arise within a learning group. The influence of that leader and how he or she thinks can affect the philosophy of the group as a whole. The leader can subtly shift the behavior of the learning group and may be able to impact the hidden curriculum as effectively as the teacher of that curriculum. If there are multiple strong personalities within the learning group, conflict can arise within the group, causing discord and a failure of any social agenda within the overall hidden curriculum.

Student learning styles need to be taken into consideration, and careful understanding of how any hidden curriculum could negatively impact training effectiveness needs to be evaluated. Faculty development is also an important consideration in making positive changes. According to Bligh (2005), "The principal purpose of faculty development is to improve practice. We use faculty development to manage change and to develop strengths and skills. This is achieved through changes in the ways people think about what they do and in changes to what they do in their work." If the underlying theories in the hidden curriculum can be found ineffective, development of the faculty may reveal new and better theories for the hidden curriculum, but only if the faculty has the knowledge and skills to suggest the appropriate changes.

Caution has to be taken in that novice problem-based learning students try to solve problems too quickly without analyzing most probable causes. Only through the analysis of the problem are critical thinking skills and knowledge acquired.

Some researchers believe that the presence of group members can sometimes restrict idea generation.
Arts, Gijselaers, and Segers (2006) suggest that individual members of a group should brainstorm solutions before the learning group gathers together for group sessions. Thus the first stage of brainstorming consists of individual preparation followed by group discussion. After the brief presentation of the topic to the general audience, individual group members should take a few

minutes to think of possible solutions to that topic, case study, or question before the group discussions begin.

Trainers may not have the authority to change the program format.
Trainers need to either have the authority or be able to acquire the authority to make this paradigm shift from classic lecture to small group, problem-based learning. In some organizations, the training department reports to marketing; in others, it reports into sales. In either case, trainers need to make sure stakeholders from both areas are involved in the inception of the product training strategy. Only by obtaining buy-in from stakeholders in authority will this (and any) training program be successful.

Training managers need to have, or obtain, the authority to promote strategic change.

Logistical Issues

Logistical concerns can inhibit change during product training planning sessions. Training logistics, if taken into account early in the strategic process, will not become an issue.

Changing a training room from a classic lecture format to small learning groups can be easy, depending on the underlying room setup.
Some corporate training departments use amphitheaters to conduct training; additional budget considerations may need to be thought of in this situation. Alternatives to the one classroom, small group format may need to be addressed. Creation of a plan and budget to physically change the training room to accommodate small learning groups may be necessary.

Identifying training venue needs is important.
Most corporations use an outside agency to obtain venues for large product training events. Discussing the small group format need with the appropriate people well in advance of training will save headache and potentially a lot of money. Contracting a large ballroom takes at least five to six months in popular cities. And believe it or not, all stakeholders usually have different ideas as to their city of preference. Of course, the stakeholder that holds the training budget has the last word, but I have found that everyone needs to be listened to.

Investing in an LMS can be expensive.
Most large companies do have a learning management system; for those that don't, I suggest the investment. Not only can an LMS be used for product training but all employee training and even customer training can be better organized and tracked.

Product inventory numbers may not meet the needs of the new training program.

Since each learning group requires a sample of the product that is to be trained on, product inventory may need to be increased to accommodate the learning group strategy. Products for new product training can usually be borrowed from engineering, marketing, or sales.

It may appear at first that the number of challenges in implementing this paradigm shift is daunting. However, the solutions in implementing this paradigm shift are simple and straightforward—you plan, plan, plan and communicate, communicate, communicate—just like you would for any other product training program.

Chapter 9:

THE FUTURE OF LEARNING

Major changes are predicted for the next decade relative to adult education and distance learning. As technology evolves, so will learning, thus distance learning will evolve as the primary method of educating adults. There will be less brick and mortar schooling and more education via e-learning technologies, whether computer-based or Web-based training. We can see much of this change happening now. In the future, distance learning will be the primary mode of delivering education.

The next generation of learners will have grown up with the advanced technology needed to ensure rapid acceptance of distance learning programs. We all have witnessed that technology has evolved over the last generation and dramatically over the last few years to provide state-of-the-art learning programs from a multitude of locations. For corporate learning, computer- and Web-based technology has allowed for an explosion in the numbers and types of learning programs that the global employee can participate in outside of the traditional walls of a classroom. Much of the training that is today provided via face-to-face classrooms will (in the not too distant future) be provided over the Web.

We are in a global learning environment. Both computer-based training (CBT) and Web-based training (WBT) will evolve to offer a multitude of both synchronous and asynchronous learning programs. Many distance education programs are currently asynchronous and will continue to be so. Benefits of asynchronous programs include the student being able to access the program whenever he or she desires. Strategies that will work best in this environment include the formation of learning groups to facilitate interactivity—proof that small group, problem-based learning will continue into the future. Projects are completed in small teams that discuss varying points of view in addressing educational issues. Since more independence is expected and required in an online environment, main forum discussions can ensure that a variety of viewpoints can be identified and discussed. Discussion questions, delivered by the instructor, ensure that the discussion topics relate to the course objectives. This is an example of a true learning community.

The rapidly growing global community will necessitate the dominance of e-learning strategies.

Distance learning strategies that are synchronous include those programs that provide education at a specific time but that take place in different locations. In the distance learning environment, several programs would meet this strategy. One such program is a webinar, or a seminar on the Web, where an interactive presentation can be combined with a "talking head" and a live chat room. Webinars are advertised and broadcast at specific times. Another example of a synchronous distance learning program is videoconferencing. The technology has been around for quite a while to implement this type of program and the cost has come down significantly. Videoconferencing is a way to bring synchronicity to a distance learning initiative.

Virtual classrooms will become the norm in the future. Virtual classrooms will be easy to access in the next decade as technologies drive acceleration of better videoconferencing solutions. Those adults that enjoy the social aspects of learning but cannot afford the time or cost to travel to the classroom will embrace a real-time classroom experience where the teacher and students are visualized together. Teachers will act more as facilitators of learning rather than as instructors. Task-based learning will be the standard, incorporating learning applications into the instruction. As technology improves (and it is improving fast), product training will be able to be performed in regional and local training centers throughout the world. This is a much more cost-effective way to train than to fly people to a central location. Instruction will be broadcast via live transmission with training facilitators providing local support. All face-to-face training programs can be accomplished in this fashion.

In many educational institutions, the LMS is used as a training portal and is where all technology is housed to deliver, archive, and track instruction. Some type of LMS is essential to the future of any learning organization, whether the LMS is housed in a central location or the Web and used independently as a portal.

It would be an excellent idea to investigate acquiring an LMS *now* if you don't have one. It's going to be the key to your learning future. At least think about what type of learning portal you will need.

Instruction may evolve to be more individualized and student-centered. The theory of independence in distance learning asserts that students should have priority with choice of objectives, how they will study, and how they are evaluated. Students are in the center of the learning process and are in charge of how they would learn and even the activities to facilitate learning. According to Saba (2003), "The centrality of the learner is one of the distinguishing features of distance education, and understanding this fact is essential for discerning why it is essentially different from other forms of education". The theory of industrialization stresses the structure of distance learning and its impact on the learning process (Chaney, 2006). The emergence of the need for education programs to reach a mass audience is also included within this theory. In this theory, the curriculum and delivery method must be standardized in order to be effective. Developing distance learning in a methodological manner increases efficiencies and decreases cost. The Internet has created a "post-industrial viewpoint." The theory of independence is very different from the industrialization theory because the position of the learner (student) is central in the independence theory and peripheral in the industrialization theory.

The theory of interaction and communication revolves around how the student will be stimulated through the distance learning environment. Since the learning is centered around the student, this theory is similar to the independence theory. The interaction is provided through the course materials; interaction can be provided one-on-one through chat rooms and videolinks. Group interaction and communication is also provided through chat rooms, as well as in discussion groups. It is important to establish a bond, or rapport, between student and facilitator because motivation plays a key role in student participation and satisfaction.

Direct connection to the Internet will be widely used for education, but alternative learning delivery methods will abound for those not wired. Mobile learning devices, used currently for entertainment purposes, will be accessible for everyone and be more widely used. Distance education delivery through everyday communication technologies such as television will be an easy avenue for the average adult to access learning.

Many Gen X and Gen Y people will have grown up on computer gaming. Simulations will prove to be a primary method to learn new skills. This realistic learning tool will replace many linear delivery technologies. Simulations provide a more active engagement for all learners, including the adult.

Instant messaging and podcasting is starting to become a delivery mechanism for mobile learning. While not an option that will replace virtual classrooms or more encompassing instruction, mobile learning is proving to provide instant access to valuable educational information. The density of instruction will change as the information is "chunked" into usable five- to ten-minute learning segments. With this change in instructional strategy, students can access the information needed at the particular time it is needed. For example, someone on a business trip who needs to talk to a customer about a new product can access a five-minute podcast on the top points to make to the customer in talking about the new product.

Blogging and wikis are increasingly becoming a normal way of distance communication. Learners are forming huge communities where they can interact educationally and socially; this will only increase in the future. More group and individual mentoring programs will arise from the discussions within the learning communities. Group support of individual goals will help to ensure individual success.

Learning institutions will partner with each other and the corporate world to provide easy access for adult distance learning programs. Corporations can outsource employee education needs to those individuals and institutions that are expert in adult learning solutions.

The entire corporate workplace will be transformed by the utilization of future learning technologies. Global e-learning solutions are expensive, but the long-term benefits to reaching employees anywhere are enormous. The decreased need for employees to gather in a central location for training purposes means a huge cost savings for the company. Continued learning through the implementation of computer-based training or virtual classrooms means that the employee is current on knowledge. Instant information can be provided to any employee in the world through mobile learning. The result will be realized as increased productivity for the global corporate workforce.

Conclusion

Over 90 percent of the sales representatives and all the sales managers at my last employer appreciated the small group, problem-based learning approach because they realized the value in the addition of discussion groups and the use of real-life customer case studies. The movement away from the passive style of the large audience format was seen as a positive tactic. The incorporation of small group learning teams enhanced the problem-based learning strategy because the small group discussions enhanced learning.

Results from assessments confirmed that the implementation of small group, problem-based learning techniques into the product training classes increased the competence and confidence of sales team members in communicating product features, functions, and benefits to customers in a solutions approach to selling that customers related to.

Management realizes that product training is not a one-time event. Using a blended learning technique to product training in a phased approach not only provides efficient, flexible ways for employees to obtain knowledge, but it also increases retention of learned information.

Any company can implement these strategies within their learning organization. Moving to this new paradigm shift in training, with its proven benefits, will prove to be a long-term competitive advantage.

Bibliography

Arts, J. A. R., Gijselaers, W. H., & Segers, M. S. R. (2006). Enhancing problem-solving expertise by means of an authentic, collaborative, computer supported and problem-based course. *European Journal of Psychology of Education,* 21 (1), 71–90. Retrieved January 28, 2007, from EBSCO host database.

Attia, A. M., Honeycutt, E. D., & Leach, M. P. (2005). A three-stage model for assessing and improving sales force training and development. *Journal of Personal Selling and Sales Management,* 25 (3), 253–268. Retrieved April 21, 2006, from EBSCO host database.

Azer, S. A. (2005). Challenges facing PBL tutors: 12 tips for successful group facilitation. *Medical Teacher,* 27 (8), 676–681. Retrieved January 28, 2007, from EBSCO host database.

Bandura, A. (2002). Social cognitive theory in cultural context. *Applied Psychology: an International Review,* 51 (2), 269–290. Retrieved June 4, 2006, from EBSCO host database.

Brewer, S. A., Klein, J. D., & Mann, K. E. (2003). Using small group learning strategies with adult re-entry students. *College Student Journal,* 37 (2), 286–297. Retrieved April 21, 2006, from EBSCO host database.

Browder, D. M., Spooner, F., Wakeman, S., Trela, K., & Baker, J. N. (2006). Aligning Instruction With Academic Content Standards: Finding the Link. *Research & Practice for Persons with Severe Disabilities,* 31 (4), 309–321. Retrieved June 14, 2007, from EBSCO Host database.

Campbell, K. S., Davis, L., & Skinner, L. (2006). Rapport management during the exploration phase of the salesperson: Customer relationship. *Journal of Personal Selling & Sales Management,* 26 (4), 359–370. Retrieved February 10, 2007, from EBSCO host database.

Chaney, B. H. (2006). History, Theory, and Quality Indicators of Distance Education: A Literature Review. Retrieved August 8, 2007 from http://ohi.tamu.edu/distanceed.pdf

Choi, J. N., Price, R. H., & Vinokur, A. D. (2003). Self-efficacy changes in groups: effects of diversity, leadership, and group climate. *Journal of Organizational Behavior,* 24 (4), 357–72. Retrieved January 20, 2007, from EBSCO host database.

Crosby, J. R., & Hesketh, E. A. (2004). Snippets on small group learning. *Medical Teacher,* 26 (1), 16–19. Retrieved from Retrieved January 17, 2006, from EBSCO host database.

David, C. (2006). Revving up eLearning to drive sales. *EContent,* 29 (2), 28–32. Retrieved February 10, 2007, from EBSCO host database.

De Villiers, M., Bresick, G., & Mash, B. (2003). The value of small group learning: an evaluation of an innovative CPD programme for primary care medical practitioners. *Medical Education,* 37, 815–821. Retrieved April 21, 2006, from EBSCO host database.

Dochy, F., Segers, M., Van den Bossche, P., & Gijbels, D. (2003). Effects of problem-based learning: a meta-analysis *Learning and Instruction,* 13, 533–568. Retrieved February 10, 2007 from http://www.elearning reviews.org/topics/pedagogy/communication/2003-dochy-et-al. effects-problem-based-learning/.

Ewing, T. (2003). Aligning instruction to standards: a local approach. *Leadership,* 32 (3), 30–32. Retrieved June 14, 2007, from EBSCO Host database.

Gitomer, J. (2006) Sales 'objections' don't exist. *Inside Tucson Business,* 16 (25), 30. Retrieved February 10, 2007, from EBSCO host database.

Farmer, E. A., & Page, G.(2005). A practical guide to assessing clinical decision-making skills using the key features approach. *Medical Education,* 39 (12), 1188–1194. Retrieved January 28, 2007, from EBSCO host database.

Fenwick, T. J. (2002). Problem-based learning, group process and the mid-career professional: implications for graduate education. *Higher Education Research and Development,* 21 (1), 5–21. Retrieved April 21, 2006, from EBSCO host database.

Hahn, L. (2006). Tuning Up Sales Skills. *Sales & Marketing Management,* 158 (2), pg. 17. Retrieved February 10, 2007, from EBSCO host database.

Hall, B. (2005). Sales Training Makeovers. *Training,* 42 (5), 15–20. Retrieved April 24, 2006, from EBSCO host database.

Hayes, D. (2003). Making learning an effect of schooling: aligning curriculum, assessment and pedagogy. *Discourse: Studies in the Cultural Politics of Education,* 24 (2) 225–246. Retrieved June 14, 2007, from EBSCO Host database.

Hunt, D. P., Haidet, P., Coverdale, J. H., & Richards, B. (2002). The effect of using team learning in an evidence-based medicine course for medical students. *Teaching and Learning in Medicine,* 15(2), 131–39. Retrieved April 21, 2006 from EBSCO host database.

Kasuya, R. T. (2004). Give your audience a problem and they will listen. *Presentation.* Retrieved May 3, 2006, from InfoTrac OneFile via Thomson Gale: http://find.galegroup.com/itx/infomark. do?&contentSet=IAC-Documents&type=retrieve&tabID=T002&p rodId=ITOF&docId=A120846780&source=gale&userGroupNam e=uphoenixc.

Massaro, F. J., Harrison, M. R., & Soares, A. (2006). Use of problem-based learning in staff training and development. *American Journal of Health-System Pharmacy,* 63 (22), 2256–2259. Retrieved January 28, 2007, from EBSCO host database.

Miflin, B. (2004). Small groups and problem-based learning: are we singing from the same hymn sheet? *Medical Teacher,* 26 (5), 444–450. Retrieved April 22, 2006, from EBSCO host database.

Naughton, J. (2008). IOL: Determining the impact of learning. *Chief Learning Officer,* 7 (9). 32–37.

Nieminen, J., Sauri, P., & Lonka, K. (2006). On the relationship between group functioning and study success in problem-based learning. *Medical Education,* 40 (1), 64–71. Retrieved January 28, 2007, from EBSCO host database.

Pearlman, B. (2006). Twenty-first century learning in schools: A case study of New Technology High School in Napa, California. *New Directions for Youth Development,* (110), 101–112. Retrieved January 28, 2007, from EBSCO host database.

Raucent, B. (2001). Introducing problem-based learning in a machine design curriculum: result of an experiment. *Journal of Engineering Design,* 12 (4), 293–308. Retrieved April 22, 2006, from EBSCO host database.

Raymond, B. (2006). A confidence boost. *Sales & Marketing Management,* 158 (8). Retrieved February 10, 2007, from EBSCO host database.

Santanello, C., & Hildebrandt, M. (2005). The use of critical incident cases in classrooms. *Academic Exchange Quarterly,* 9, 139–144. Retrieved May 3, 2006 from InfoTrac OneFile via Thomson Gale: http://find. galegroup.com/itx/infomark.do?&contentSet=IAC-Documents&ty pe=retrieve&tabID=Too2&prodId=ITOF&docId=A142636405&s ource=gale&userGroupName=uphoenixc.

Shavelson, R. J. (2007). Assessing Student Learning Responsibly: From History to an Audacious Proposal. Change, 37 (1), 26–33. Retrieved June 28, 2007, from EBSCO host database.

Sungur, S., & Tekkaya, C. (2006). Effects of problem-based learning and traditional instruction on self-regulated learning. *Journal of Educational Research*, 99 (5), 307–317. Retrieved January 28, 2007, from EBSCO host database.

Sungur, S., Tekkaya, C., & Geban, O. (2006). Improving achievement through problem-based learning. *Journal of Biological Education*, 40 (4), 155–160. Retrieved January 28, 2007, from EBSCO host database.

Taylor, C. S., & Nolen, S. B. (2005). *Classroom assessment: Supporting teaching and learning in real classrooms.* Upper Saddle River, New Jersey: Prentice-Hall.

Vega, Q. C., & Taylor, M. R. (2005). Incorporating course content while fostering a more learner-centered environment. *College Teaching*, 53 (2), 83–86. Retrieved January 17, 2007, from EBSCO host database.

Webster, B. (2006). Knowing what they know. *Pharmaceutical Executive Supplement*, 8–12. Retrieved January 28, 2007, from EBSCO host database.

Wheeler, S. (2006). Learner support needs in online problem-based learning. *Quarterly Review of Distance Education*, 7 (2), 175–183. Retrieved January 28, 2007, from EBSCO host database.

Willis, S. C., Jones, A., Bundy, C., Burdett, K., Whitehouse, C. R., & O'Neill, P. A. (2002). Small-group work and assessment in a PBL curriculum: a qualitative and quantitative evaluation of student perceptions of the process of working in small groups and its assessment. *Medical Teacher*, 24 (5), 495–501. Retrieved February 10, 2007, from EBSCO host database.

Winfrey, E. C. (1999). Kirkpatrick's Four Levels of Evaluation. In B. Hoffman (Ed.), *Encyclopedia of Educational Technology*. Retrieved March 8, 2007, from http://coe.sdsu.edu/eet/articles/k4levels/start.htm

Appendix A:

AN OVERVIEW OF THE ADDIE MODEL OF INSTRUCTIONAL DESIGN

Instructional design is simply the process of selecting learning materials and content in a way to transfer knowledge in the most efficient manner possible. Many processes for instructional design exist. One systematic process for instructional design is the ADDIE model. This model approaches design almost linearly, from analysis, design, development, implementation, and evaluation. There are many types of ADDIE models, but all use generally the same process. The simple model used by this author consists of five "phases" of a curricular project: analysis, design, development, implementation, and evaluation.

Analysis

The analysis phase ensures that the program will be valid—it will deliver what it is meant to deliver. The analysis phase is to define and clarify what instructional problem a curriculum would address. Goals and objectives for the instructional program fall out of this analysis, as do learner characteristics and environment. The purpose of the analysis phase is to determine what content and type of learning program would best meet the needs of the learner. The length of the analysis phase depends upon the project complexity and learner characteristics.

Design

The design phase of a program consists of evaluation of the delivery vehicle best suited for the learner needs. Strategies for delivery of instruction are decided along with the type(s) of media that will be used. Most classroom programs will be designed with the small group format of instruction in mind. The design phase is based off the analysis and the determined needs.

Development

The development phase implements the decisions made in the design phase. The development of the program is also based on the analysis because learner characteristics and needs assessment may drive the type of program development. For example, visual learners will need visual backup during lectures.

Implementation

Implementation usually consists of three phases. The first phase is a pilot program consisting of a small target audience to test the curriculum delivery. The second phase is a "train the trainer" session facilitated by the training manager(s) to ensure successful implementation by any or all end trainers. The third phase is the final delivery of the curriculum by the trainer. Depending on the formative evaluation outcome, the pilot program may be greatly reduced or eliminated.

The implementation stage depends on the development and analysis. For example, in distance learning programs, the use of multimedia may be needed to provide better examples of the program content.

Evaluation

Lastly, any program needs to have both formative and summative evaluations performed. Formative evaluation is used during the design and development of a program. The purpose of formative evaluation is to ensure that the instructional goals are valid. Formative evaluation is performed using a small group of people to view or even run a trial of the curriculum. Usually the target audience consists of end-users of the curriculum. Formative evaluation implementation for the Five Phase training model is discussed in more depth in chapter 5.

Summative evaluation determines whether the program accomplished the stated goals by assessing learning achievement. This type of evaluation looks at groups of students to determine trends. For example, if most students did not do well on a section of test or assessment, a revision may be made to the curriculum in the design or delivery. Learner feedback in the form of a survey is also part of summative evaluation. Summative evaluation implementation for the Five Phase training model is discussed in more depth in chapter 5.

Using a systematic method for instructional design is highly recommended over the use of informal models for several reasons. Processes that are systematic allow for smoother development of training programs with less chance of problems. This is especially important for technology-based training programs using blended (both classroom and distance) learning delivery systems. Efficiency can be vital when developing distance learning programs, which can be much costlier than regular classroom programs due to the increased use of technology and incorporation and maintenance of an LMS. The risk of some needed component being lost in communication is greatly reduced if a systematic way to design instruction is used. Using a formula that has been proven to succeed just makes more sense than making one up.

Appendix B:

An Overview of Kirkpatrick Levels of Learning

Evaluating students to assess their level of learning is essential in not only proving training's value to upper management, but also in making sure the students were taught and learned what they needed in order to succeed, whether that student is a human resources employee or a sales representative. Unfortunately, many program evaluations consist of a program evaluation in the form of a survey. A survey in itself is useful but not predictive of actual learning. Thus, a model for learning evaluation needs to be adopted and followed. Perhaps the best known model for evaluating learning is Kirkpatrick's Four Levels of Evaluation, developed by Donald Kirkpatrick (Winfrey 1999).

The first level is evaluation. Simply put, this level measures to what extent the students were satisfied with a particular training program. A survey is a generally accepted mode of collecting and disseminating this information. The program survey asks the students what they liked about the program and what they would do to improve upon the course. Many call this the "smile sheet." According to Kirkpatrick (Winfrey 1999), all programs need to be evaluated at least at this level to ensure the capability to improve future courses. It is important to note that the Four Levels model is built upon the assumption that each level needs to be attained to reach the next.

The first level is needed for progression to the second level of learning, which is called the learning level. For example, a test given at the conclusion of a training program is performed to assess the skill level of the student(s) in meeting knowledge requirements. To some, the "Learning" level suggests that a pre and post-test needs to be completed to ensure learning has progressed (Winfrey 1999).

The third level, transfer, assesses students at the level that they interact with their environment. In the sales environment, the question to be asked is, "Is the salesperson using the knowledge they gained during training and applying it to the sales situation?" It is this measure that would bring the best measure of the training's impact. Understanding how product features and benefits help solve customer problems is measured at this level. Performance-based assessments are used at this level, as well as documentation of application in real-life situations. I firmly believe that the success of all product training programs should be based on the accomplishment of all three of these levels.

The fourth level, results, is generally not directly measured in the majority of learning organizations. Results mean that the bottom line has been addressed; in the sales environment that equates to increased sales. As we all know, many variables impact sales; training is one that is difficult and expensive, but not impossible, to measure. However, in times of economic uncertainty, the fourth level may be used more frequently as a way to prove training value to executive management.

More on the Kirkpatrick levels of evaluation can be found at http://coe.sdsu.edu/eet/articles/k4levels/start.htm.

Appendix C:

USING MODELING IN LEARNING

Modeling is an important concept of Albert Bandura's (2002) social cognitive theory of learning and can be found in both pedagogical and andragogical learning environments. Modeling is a process of behavior modification where one student "models" the behavior of another person. Modeling not only provides the opportunity to teach new behaviors but also to increase the frequency that the student uses that behavior. For example, inexperienced students such as salespeople can learn how to present product value more easily from observing and mimicking the more experienced employee within discussion groups.

New and pertinent ways of presenting data to a customer will change an employee's behavior in a significant way. For example, some sales representatives feel that all they need to do is to recite technological differences to the customer in order to get the sale. They often fail when behaving in this manner. In new-hire or product training, they should be taught skills to relate the technologies to the customer in a way that customers can relate to and see the benefits to them. This technique of presenting the product value to customers results in a higher likelihood of a sale. Modeling is an important concept in the sales training environment, and it is a cornerstone of many classroom training programs.

Four steps are seen in the process of modeling behavior. The first step is "attention." If one does not pay attention, learning will not occur. If a student is not interested in the instructor or the content there is little attention paid to the content. If the model is interesting to students, they will be more likely to pay attention. For example, if the instructor has an interesting accent, increased attention may be noted from the audience. Because there will be didactic lectures (both in classroom and distance learning), continued student attention to the presented material can be problematic. To increase attention, multimedia and interactivity are used in the PowerPoint presentations, which are as brief as possible.

The second step of modeling is "retention." Retention of the learned material is a major issue in any training program. There is much information presented during the product training sessions. Retention of the material is increased when the personal learning style of the students is taken into account. Many ways exist of practicing the art of retaining information. Learning styles come into play in this area. For example, some people are visual learners, where they learn best by seeing. PowerPoint presentations and videotaped lectures can work well. Other people are kinesthetic learners, that is, they learn best by doing. Yet other people are auditory learners. These people learn best by listening and verbalizing. Exercises are held during product training where the students have to recite back what they have learned. Thus, knowing the learning style of one's audience is necessary for adequate retention of information.

Retention of information is also increased through repetition of subject matter. Customer case studies can be reworked in ways so that the same customer situation is used but is presented differently to the discussion group. Marketing messages, because they are brief, can be reinserted into the training material throughout the training program. At the end of training, the salespeople can recite the marketing messages (customer proof statements) without effort.

The third step of modeling is reproduction. Translating the information into behavior is the central idea of this stage. This stage involves repeated practice of the behavior. For example, one can read about riding a bicycle, but until one reproduces the task (riding the bicycle), the task will not be mastered. This stage is best practiced within the small discussion group approach to learning.

Reproduction is established through hands-on sessions, where the students are required to participate in customer situation simulations. For example, a specific customer situation is provided, and the students have to think about how they would handle that situation. They then make a presentation in front of the class. Reproduction will enhance learning retention.

The last step of modeling is motivation. Internal or external forces, personal drive, a need for approval, and a desire for incentives or a sense of accomplishment all can demonstrate motivation. Motivation to hold a job and increase income thus becomes motivation to learn. This is the motivation of typical corporate sales employees—they need to learn and master skills to be competitive in the global marketplace. Motivators are perhaps central to the learning of new employees like sales representatives. Not only do they want to make a good impression to their managers (approval), but they have the inherent need to win. The salesperson's drive consists of both internal and external motivating factors. He or she wants to win for the sake of winning. Sales representatives know they need to learn significant amounts of information in order to reach their incentive—commission from the sale. To increase the motivation of new employees, they are encouraged to add their own experiences to the discussion group topics. Because of this, sometimes the curriculum is changed to accommodate those persons' techniques.

Motivation is partially dependent on personal efficacy—that is, how confident a student is in his or her abilities. Personal efficacy is the idea that people have "the power to produce desired effects by one's actions, otherwise one has little incentive to act or to persevere in the face of difficulty" (Bandura 2002). Self-efficacy affects how individuals think and therefore behave. Collective efficacy is identified by a group of people who share similar beliefs. How well these groups of people interact is determined by the strength of their shared beliefs. Placing new employees with veterans within learning groups can enhance and even rapidly increase the development of personal efficacy of that new employee.

Appendix D:

HELPFUL TEMPLATES

Sample: Survey

The following is a survey to seek information about the quality of product training from the perspective of you and your management. To complete the survey, circle or highlight the answer that seems to be most relevant for you.

Name: _____

1. The size of the class facilitates learning and discussion

Strongly agree   Agree   Neither agree/disagree   Disagree Strongly disagree

2. There was ample opportunity for "hands-on" time.

Strongly agree   Agree   Neither agree/disagree   Disagree Strongly disagree

3. I learned the new technologies in a way that I can easily relate back to the customer.

Strongly agree   Agree   Neither agree/disagree   Disagree Strongly disagree

4. There was ample opportunity to learn and discuss the positioning of each new product feature.

Strongly agree   Agree   Neither agree/disagree   Disagree Strongly disagree

5. There was adequate time for team discussion.

Strongly agree   Agree   Neither agree/disagree   Disagree Strongly disagree

6. Real-life customer situations were addressed with this training.

Strongly agree   Agree   Neither agree/disagree   Disagree Strongly disagree

7. After training I feel confident to competently present product features, functions,

and benefits.
Strongly agree   Agree   Neither agree/disagree   Disagree Strongly disagree

8. After training, I will confidently and competently explain the new features and present the product effortlessly to customers.
Strongly agree   Agree   Neither agree/disagree   Disagree Strongly disagree

9. The training will positively impact my sales numbers.
Strongly agree   Agree   Neither agree/disagree   Disagree Strongly disagree

10. I am satisfied with the training and its format.
Strongly agree   Agree   Neither agree/disagree   Disagree Strongly disagree

Comments:_____
_____
_____

Template 2: Learning Group Member Assessment Rubric

CATEGORY	4	3	2	1	Score
Product features and function	Shows a full understanding of the topic.	Shows a good understanding of the topic.	Shows a good understanding of parts of the topic.	Does not understand the topic.	
Product feature benefits	Student is able to accurately answer almost all questions posed by the instructor about the topic.	Student is able to accurately answer most questions posed by the instructor about the topic.	Student is able to accurately answer a few questions posed by the instructor about the topic.	Student is unable to accurately answer questions posed by the instructor about the topic.	
Relating benefits to customer needs	Student is completely prepared and has obviously rehearsed.	Student seems pretty prepared but might have needed a couple more rehearsals.	The student is somewhat prepared, but it is clear that rehearsal was lacking.	Student does not seem at all prepared to present.	
Demonstrates knowledge of competition	Student is able to state three reasons why X company is better than the competition clearly and concisely.	Student is able to state clearly and concisely at least two reasons why X company is better than the competition.	Student is able to state two reasons why X company is better than competition but is somewhat unclear.	Student is able to state only one reason why X company is better than competition and is not clear in this description.	
Case study	Excellent correlation of product benefits to customer problem	Good correlation of product benefits to customer problem	Some correlation of product benefits to customer problem; needs work	No correlation of product benefit to customer problem; confused	

TOTAL SCORE_____

Comments_____

_____

_____

Template 3: Survey Result

Survey Population (Members or Managers)	Survey Results			
Scale	Strongly Disagree	Disagree	Agree	Strongly Agree
1. The size of the training class facilitates learning and discussion.				
2. There was ample opportunity for hands-on time.				
3. The students learned the new technologies in a way that they can easily relate back to the customer.				
4. The students had ample opportunity to learn and discuss the positioning of the new product features.				
5. There was adequate time for team discussion.				
6. Real-life customer situations were addressed with this training.				
7. After training, the students will confidently and competently explain the new features and present the product effortlessly to customers.				
8. After training, the students will feel confident to position the product upgrade to customers in a way they can relate to.				
9. The training will positively impact sales numbers.				
10. I am satisfied with the training and its format.				

Template 4. Classroom Setup Using Small Learning Group Approach

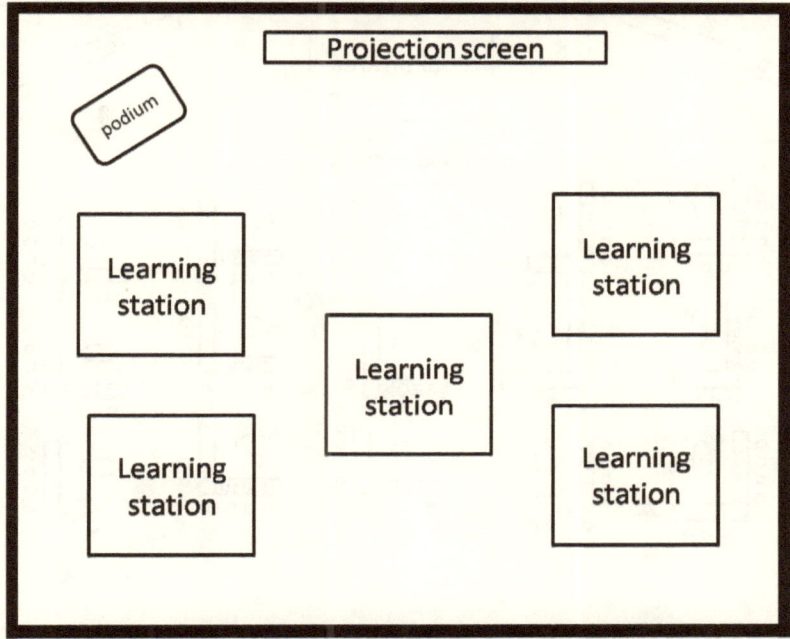

General view of classroom setup

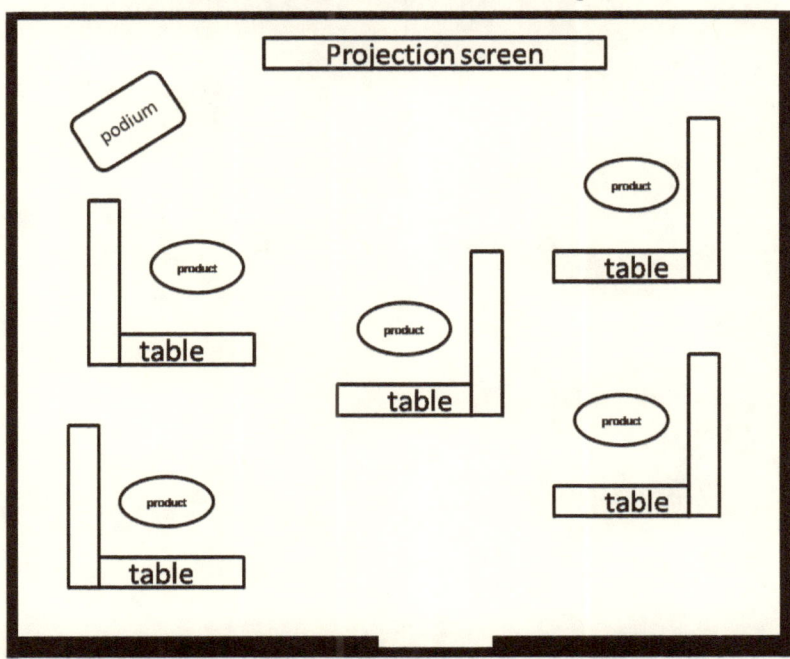

Detailed view of classroom setup

Template 5. Example of a Room Layout for New Product/Upgrade Training

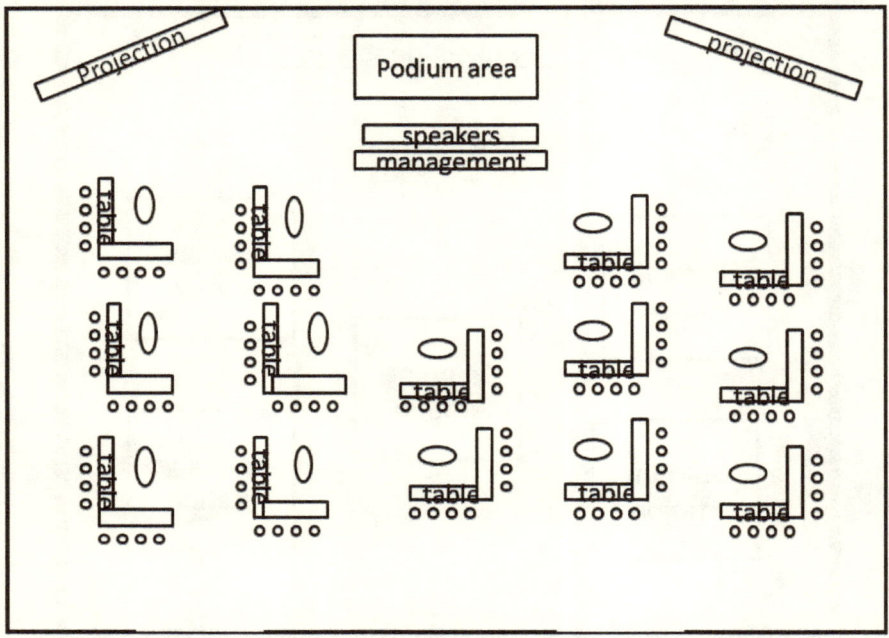